A Guide To
BACKPACKING
WITH YOUR DOG

Second Edition

Charlene G. LaBelle

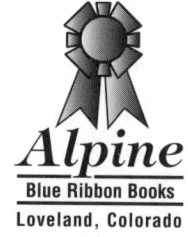

Alpine
Blue Ribbon Books
Loveland, Colorado

A Guide to Backpacking with Your Dog
Copyright © 1993, 2004 by Charlene G. LaBelle

All rights reserved. No part of this book may be used or reproduced in any manner whatsoever, including electronic media, internet, or newsletters or photocopies without written permission from the publisher, except in the case of brief quotations embodied in critical reviews. For permission, write to Alpine Publications, Inc., P. O. Box 7027, Loveland, CO 80537.

ISBN 1-57779-063-4

Library of Congress Cataloging in Publication Data

LaBelle, Charlene G.
  A guide to backpacking with your dog / Charlene G. LaBelle. -- 2nd ed.
    p. cm.
  Includes bibliographical references (p.103) and index.
  ISBN 1-57779-063-4
  1. Backpacking. 2. Dogs -- Training. I. Title: Backpacking with your dog. II. Title.

GV199.6.L33 2004
796.51 -- dc22
                            2004046418

The information contained in this book is complete and accurate to the best of our knowledge. All recommendations are made without guarantee on the part of the author or Alpine Publications, Inc. The author and publisher disclaim any liability with the use of this information.

For the sake of simplicity, the terms " he" or "she" are sometimes used to identify an animal or person. These are used in the generic sense only. No discrimination of any kind is intended toward either sex.

Many manufacturers secure trademark rights for their products. When Alpine Publications is aware of a trademark claim, we identify the product name by using initial capital letters.

This book is available at special quantity discounts for breeders and for club promotions, premiums, or educational use. Write for details.

Cover Design and Text Layout: Laura Newport
Cover Photos: (front) © Wolf Packs Inc. (back) © Judith Strom.
Photographs by the author unless otherwise indicated.

First printing of Second Edition, May 2004

1 2 3 4 5 6 7 8 9 0

Printed in the United States of America.

Contents

Preface	v
Backpacking and *Your* Dog	1
Choosing a Pack	7
Training and Conditioning	21
Planning Your First Real Trip	33
Planning Meals for You and Your Dog	45
Packing Up	55
On the Trail	65
The Mountain Bike and Your Dog	75
Taking Longer Trips	79
Geocaching—A Fun Way Hike Locally with Dogs	97
Appendix: The Dog Packer's Checklist	101
For Further Information	103
Index	109

This book is dedicated to
My first Malamute, California Golden Poppy
and
Alyeska's Kenoshka SnowBelle WPD WTD WPDX

Acknowledgements

I would like to thank: Barb Fahs; Stephen M. Schwartz, Vicky Palmer and family; Nancy Guadagna and family; Butch and Sally Meyner; Rick Meyner: Steve LaBelle; DOGSIG @ Tandem Computers; Kent and Donna Dannen; The AMCA; NCAMA; Dr. Brien Bates, DVM; and J. T.; Betty Jo McKinney for editorial assistance; Alyeska's Bearly Their WPD (Allie); Kodiak Arctic Thundercloud WPD (Kody); Glenhaven's SnoBelle WPD, WTD (Tamerack); and everyone else who supported this effort!

Preface

     I grew up backpacking with my family — my Mom, Dad, two younger brothers (Butch and Rick) and Penni (a medium-size, black-and-white Heinz).
  In 1976 I was given my first Alaskan Malamute, Poppy. I still enjoyed backpacking, and it only made sense to bring Poppy along. So, I purchased a bright orange dog pack at a swap meet at UC-Davis (Davis, California) and trained Poppy to help carry her share.
  In 1987 I purchased my first AKC registered Alaskan Malamute and became involved with the Northern California Alaskan Malamute Association (NCAMA). The NCAMAs parent club was the Alaskan Malamute Club of America (AMCA). Like many national AKC breed clubs, the AMCA has a program that recognizes working dogs. The program is designed to measure a dog's ability to perform the tasks he was specifically bred or developed to do. By meeting or exceeding certain requirements, dogs can earn a "working title." There are different rules or requirements for each of several different titles, including "sledding," "weight pulling" and "BACKPACKING!"
  At that time I was the only NCAMA member that had done much packing with dogs. I helped establish a hiking program that included dogs. Our program has grown, and together we've enjoyed lots of day hikes and a few overnighters. Soon the stories of our fun filtered to others.
  Someone on the AMCA working committee asked if I would write a brief article on backpacking with Alaskan Malamutes for the club's monthly newsletter. My first "how to" article was published there and also in the 1989-90 Winter *Malamute Quarterly*.

On July 14, 1991, while backpacking with three dogs on trail from Whitney Portal to Whitney Peak, California, I was asked for the umpteenth time in two days about a "how-to" book. "There isn't one," I replied. "I haven't written it yet."

The rest is history. So . . . If you think you and your dog would like taking trips together in the wilderness, or you are already a seasoned backpacker who would enjoy the company of your dog, this book is written for you. PLEASE, carefully train your dog BEFORE you ask him to earn his keep on the trail.

. . . Enjoy!

Charlene G. LaBelle

Author Charlene G. LaBelle with one of the first Alaskan Malamutes to be titled Working Pack Dog Excellence (WPDX) on the West Coast.

*". . . great times we had together.
Many of our best days were spent in the wilds."*

— Enos Mills, founder of Rocky Mountain National Park,
regarding his Border Collie

Author with the first Alaskan Malamutes to be titled Working Pack Dog Excellence (WPDX) on the West Coast: *(left)* Ch. Hyrum's Alaskan "Bandit" WPD WPDX; and *(right)* Alyeska's "Kenoshka" SnowBelle WPD, WTD, WPDX. This father/daughter pair were the fourth and fifth dogs to be titled WPDX in the world. This photo was taken on the 140-plus-mile trip that we took to meet the requirements of the Alaskan Malamute Club of America's Working Program and thus earn the working title of WPDX. Conard, Brokoff, and Lassen peaks in California.

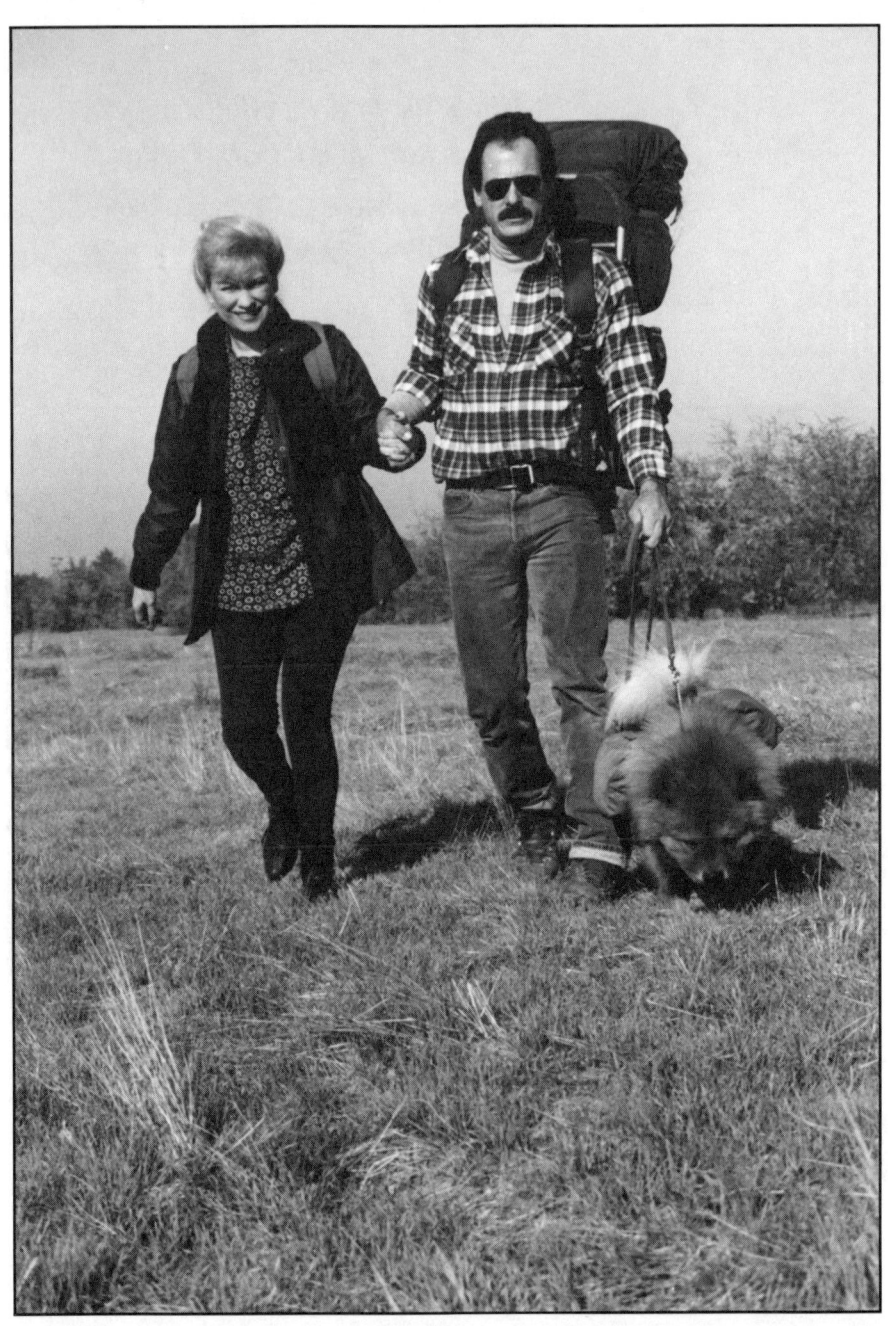
Vikki and John Palazzari hiking with Max, a one-year-old Chow.

Backpacking and *Your* Dog

Backpacking is fun — for both dogs and humans. It may encompass a one-day hike or a lengthy trip with many days and nights on the trail (overnighters). The only difference between day hiking and backpacking is that you usually carry a few more supplies when you stay overnight. Either way, taking your dogs with you means you can carry those extra items that will make your trip that much more fabulous. So, if you are already an experienced hiker who would like to utilize your dog's weight carrying ability, or if you think you and your dog might enjoy trips into the back country, this book is written for you.

Throughout this book I will tell you about my own experiences. I have hiked with dogs for over twenty years. My first four-legged companion was a medium-size "Heinz" who never "earned her keep," she just came along for the fun of it. The next series of dogs were all Alaskan Malamutes. They all earned their keep and then some. Many of my dogs have backpacked literally hundreds of miles. There have been times when, without my dogs, I would not have been able to hike.

Taking your dog with you on hikes can enrich your experience in a number of ways. There are few hiking companions as enjoyable as your dog. The communication and companionship that develops between you is difficult to duplicate in a day to day urban lifestyle. Furthermore, in the event that you are traveling with your dog, there is no need for you to be prevented from exploring the parks and forests because it is too hot or cold to leave your dog behind and no boarding facilities are available. With training and conditioning, your dog can accompany you to many areas which you might previously have had to miss.

In addition to decreasing the weight of your own pack and thereby making the trip more enjoyable, the extra space created by the dog's pack can make room for guide books, camera equipment, binoculars or other items that will increase your appreciation of nature's wonders. This extra space and weight-carrying ability afforded by the dog's pack is also valuable to hikers with small children or those with physical problems.

Dogs inflict less damage on the wilderness than any other pack animal because they eat only the food they carry and cause no erosion to the trail. Their sense of smell and hearing is much more acute than that of humans, so dogs can alert you to many birds and wildlife you might otherwise miss.

Mike Hacker with two "rescue dogs," Bo on the left, Clay on the right.

Obviously, taking your dog into parks and wilderness areas demands responsibility, good manners, and some degree of training. Dogs should always be on lead, especially when near other people, dogs, or wildlife. Aggressive or difficult to control dogs do not belong on the trail. Courtesy and responsibility will be increasingly important if more parks and recreation areas are to be persuaded to allow pack dogs on the trails. If you love the beauty and solitude of the backcountry, and love having your dog along, take the time to learn the rules, properly train and control your pet, and keep the trails clean and safe for other hikers.

WHAT KIND OF DOG CAN PACK?

Any dog that is in good physical condition and enjoys hiking with you can go backpacking. And any breed of dog — from purebred to mutt — will do nicely. However, that doesn't necessarily mean that every individual canine will make a good backpacking dog. While many dogs are fine trail (hiking) companions, not all can carry a lot of weight. Certain "packing breed" dogs may not be able or willing to carry packs, while dogs of a breed not noted for its weight carrying ability might pack exceptionally well.

As a general rule, dogs with light, short coats do better in the heat than dogs with heavy and/or long coats. Dogs with full coats are more functional when hiking in the cold. (However, a short-coated dog can wear a jacket in cold weather.) Short-coated dogs collect fewer burrs, foxtails and seeds in their coats during spring and summer hikes than do the long-coated varieties.

Before you select a dog for backpacking, carefully consider the types of trails you'll be taking, seasonal weather conditions in your area, the dog's stamina and enthusiasm, and your commitment to training and conditioning. If you often go on overnight or longer trips into the back country in rough terrain, you'll want a large, strong dog for your backpacking companion, and large, well constructed packs. On the other hand, if you occasionally go for short walks and want to carry water, a camera and some snacks, a smaller dog and a less expensive, less durable pack will do just fine.

Some breeds, like the Alaskan Malamute and Rottweiler, have been carrying packs for centuries. Others, like many of the larger sporting breeds, were not bred for packing ability, but we are seeing a lot of them on the trails and they seem to do exceptionally well. Most of the working and many of the herding breeds are able packers. It really depends on the dog. It should go without saying that a dog with temperament problems, back or leg weaknesses, or other physical problems, should not be allowed on the trails.

Barb Fahs and Amber.

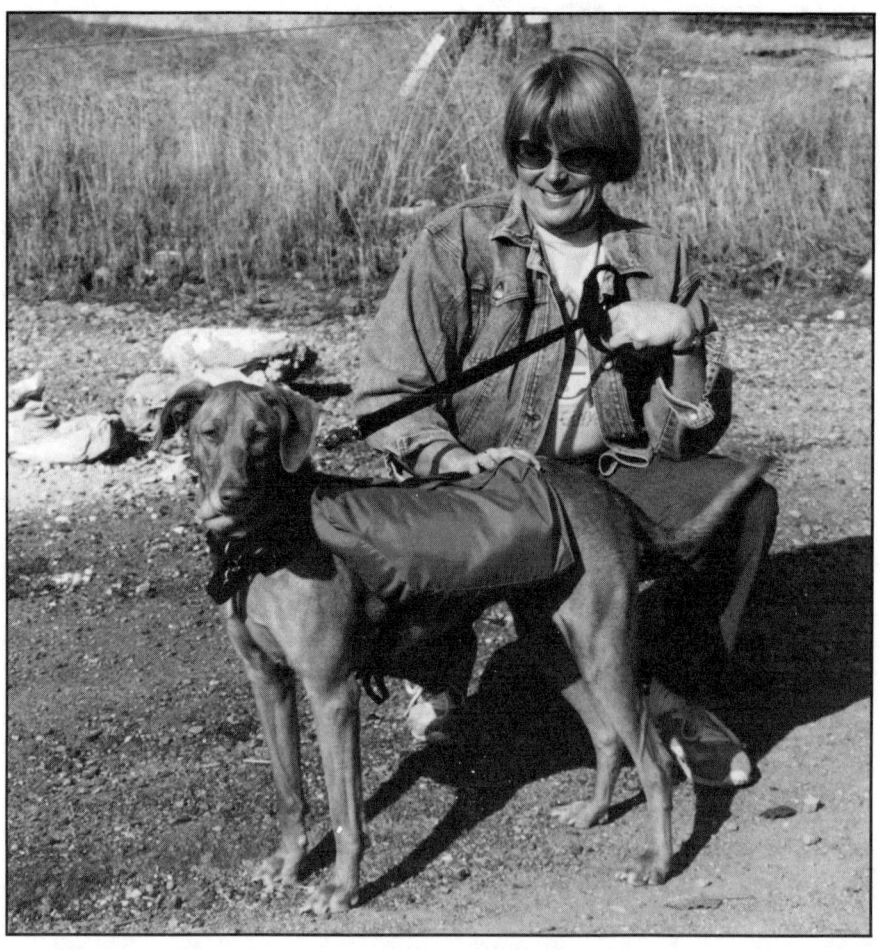

HOW MUCH CAN HE CARRY?

Every pound over the weight of his own food that your dog carries is one less pound on your back. This makes an especially great difference when you are hiking with children or those who are physically unable to carry their own share.

Most dogs, with conditioning and practice, carry approximately one-fourth of their body weight. Most "packing" breeds, when in good physical condition and on a well-balanced diet, can carry at least thirty percent of their body weight. That means a 100-pound dog can carry a 30-pound pack over long periods of time with no signs of fatigue. Our experienced 90- to 100-pound Malamutes usually begin a trip carrying 35 or 36 pounds. These dogs, when in top shape, can easily pack up to fifty percent of their body weight.

WHAT SPECIAL EQUIPMENT DO I NEED?

The three basic items you need to take your dog backpacking are: (1) a 6- to 8-foot leash, (2) a collar and (3) a quality dog pack. Other essentials for your dog include clean water, snacks, flea and tick repellant, plus food, water and food pans, and a stake-out chain for overnight trips. (See page 55 for a list of other suggested items.)

Let's start with the leash and collar. There is no reason to go out and buy a new leash and collar. A leather leash is easy on your hands, but a nylon one works just fine. A piece of rope with a comfortable handle can be very functional. I use an 8-foot piece of nylon rope with a handle like the one you would find on a water ski rope. Longer leashes or *Flexi-leads* are acceptable in some areas, while other park requirements specify a six-foot leash. Think of the leash as a safety device. The leash will help you to protect your dog from porcupines, snakes, skunks and other wildlife you do not want him to meet at close range. A leash is almost a guarantee that you will always have control of the situation. And, since some people or animals you meet may be afraid of dogs, keeping your dog leashed helps assure you of the good will of your fellow hikers, bike and horseback riders, and llama packers.

My dogs wear one-inch-wide nylon web collars because I like the security of using thicker collars. I frequently have a second collar on the dog — a training collar or choke chain. Never allow a dog to run loose when wearing a choke collar. It could get caught in the brush and strangle him.

Choose a collar style and width that is comfortable and secure for your dog. A rolled leather collar is a good choice for long-coated breeds because it doesn't damage the coat. A current rabies tag and an ID tag with your name, address, and telephone number should always be attached to the collar. It is always a good idea to carry a spare leash and collar.

Packs with pads, leashes, and water bucket.

Choosing a Pack

WHAT EXACTLY IS A DOG PACK?

A dog pack is made up of two compartments (pack, panniers, pouches or saddle bags) in which the dog can carry items. These packs are attached via a yoke or pad placed over the dog's shoulders. The packs (containers) are most commonly made in one of three shapes: square or box shape, saddle bag or "U" shape, or contour. The square (box) shape is probably the most common and fits the most gear.

The most important things to remember when selecting a pack are that it must properly fit your dog and it should be suitable for the type of hiking you plan to do. Then, purchase a quality pack. Don't compromise on quality to save money.

Some companies that make great dog packs also sell marginal packs. Check with local outdoor or camping equipment stores to see if they carry dog packs. Many of the larger pet stores also carry them. If you can't find a pack locally, you can always mail order (see appendices), but be sure to return the pack if it doesn't fit properly.

If possible, take your dog with you when you go to purchase a pack. If you have a puppy you are considering training to pack, wait until he has reached his adult size before buying a pack. That way you won't need to purchase another, larger pack as he grows.

Most packs are sized according to a dog's weight. They usually are available in small size (30 to 50 pounds), medium (50 to 75 pounds), large (75 to 100 pounds), and extra large (for dogs over

square/box saddlebag/"U" contour

100 pounds). The average cost is between twenty and seventy-five dollars, depending upon size and quality.

Packs are available in many shapes, colors and designs. In addition, there are one, two, and even three piece packs. Cheaper packs may have only two straps, while the better ones have three or four straps to hold the pack in place.

Whatever pack you decide upon, I cannot stress too strongly the importance of selecting one made of quality materials, the proper size and fit for your dog. A poorly fitted pack can injure your dog's back or legs. If the packs sags, it will rub the dog's elbows until they are raw. A pack that is too narrow will sit on top of the dog's back and wear the coat, or even cause sores on his back. Zippers can break if the pack is poorly constructed, or, still worse, the bottom of the pack can wear through, spilling the contents on the trail.

TYPES OF PACKS

One-Piece Packs

Many of the lightweight, one-piece packs have a narrow yoke and smaller compartments. These packs fit perfectly well on small dogs with narrow backs, and they are great for day hikes. They won't fit Malamutes or any other breed with a wide back, and the pack space is quite small. If you plan on taking extended trips, buy a heavier pack. But, if you plan to day hike and only need to carry your lunch, water and a few small items, the one-piece nylon packs

BIS multi Intl/Am CH. Belle's Cool Holiday Special WWPD, WPD, CGC, TT, CACIB, CAC, CACH, CACH-B, CACH-S, owned by Charlene LaBelle, wears a dog pack from Wolf Packs.

A one-piece pack, contour in shape with a mesh yoke.

will do nicely. The better ones have three straps, and many have a place at the back where you can attach your leash.

Some one-piece packs are available in heavy-duty material. These fit the same and look the same as the two-piece packs, except that the pad is part of the pack. They come with three straps and a D-ring or loop at the center of the rear edge of the back piece.

Two-Piece Packs

A large, durable two-piece pack is the appropriate choice if you plan on making backpacking with your dog a frequent and significant activity. The pad, or yoke, of the two-piece pack is held in place by three straps. The pad, which may be contoured to fit the shape of the dog's back, is constructed from padded canvas, nylon webbing, or nylon mesh. Some are adjustable. The better ones have soft webbing protectors at all pressure points.

The yoke should reflect the size of the dog. The larger the dog, the wider the yoke. A correctly fitted yoke will allow the panniers to hang straight down to or just slightly below the dog's belly. It will distribute the weight of the packs evenly, insuring the dog's comfort. If the yoke is too narrow, the packs cannot be completely filled and will look as if they are riding on top of the dog's back. They will be difficult to balance and may wear sores on the back. If the yoke is too wide, the packs will sag and bump into the dog's legs as he walks.

Two-piece packs weigh a little more, but the pad offers extra protection and heavier material is used in their construction. Therefore, it takes the dog longer to wear out this pack. (Yes, I have had dogs wear out packs!).

I have several two-piece packs with different size packs. While I fit only one pad per dog, and he always wears the same pad, I may change the packs or panniers. I prefer the two-piece packs because I can remove the weight at lunch stops, leaving only the pad on the dog. Also, I leave the pads on overnight in camp to help identify my "wolf-grey" Malamutes as dogs. The pads can provide warmth in cold weather, too.

Look for pouches that are easy to detach, pack and clean. Most are made of nylon because it combines light weight with durability. Panniers are fastened to the yoke with velcro strips or buckles, or both. Again, look for quality construction: double stitching, seam

Choosing a Pack   11

Square/box pack. Note: "D" rings are strategically placed for attaching gear to outside of pack.

Pad for a two-piece pack.

A smaller contour-shaped, two-piece pack.

binding, double zippers or at least double sliders, flaps to protect the zippers. Zippers should be of self-healing nylon.

Some panniers come with straps or ties for attaching items to the outside of the pack.

On top of the yoke, look for D-rings, loops, tie-ons, or daisy chains. These extras will expand the dimensions and usefulness of the pack by allowing you to lash on your tent or tarp.

STRAPS AND FASTENERS

The backpack should have at least three straps, a chest strap and two belly straps, to secure the pack on the dog. One strap goes across the chest in front of the forelegs. A second strap fits just behind the front legs like the girth on a saddle, and the third strap angles back towards the flank. I have also used packs with a fourth strap which goes around the rump under the tail. This fourth strap is only needed when you're climbing or hiking in really rough country (and I'm not sure it does much good then).

Some packs are joined together at the top with mesh; others have adjustable straps with D-rings or buckles. On a few models the panniers are separate, actually forming a three-piece pack.

If I purchase a pack with adjustable D-rings holding the packs, the first thing I do is replace them with buckles. I feel D-rings are too difficult to fasten and rarely stay tightened or secure. Another reason that I dislike them is because they are usually made of metal and can freeze up in cold weather. At the end of a long trip you will appreciate anything that makes simple tasks easier. Quick release buckles (or Fastex fasteners) can be substituted for the D-rings, making it very easy to put the pack on and take it off. Sometimes you need to remove a pack quickly, such as when crossing deep streams, or if a dog should get hung up in brush.

The front strap may have velcro tabs to help secure the edge of the packs to the pad. A wide strip of velcro running down the center of the yoke, with a matching strip on the centerpiece between the packs, will help keep the packs secure.

BRUSH STRAPS

Many packs come equipped with brush straps — a 10 to 12 foot long strap that is used to keep the packs in place. The brush strap is threaded through the D-rings on the pack and completely encircles dog and packs several times. Using a brush strap makes quick removal of the pouches next to impossible, so I prefer not to use them. I have had to remove packs quickly, like the time one of my dogs attempted to jump a three-foot retaining wall. She made it, but her pack got caught in the brush. I quickly removed the pack, freeing her. If the pack had been secured with a brush strap, she would have ended up dangling from the brush, struggling, while I attempted to unwrap the strap. Just imagine attempting to unthread the brush strap from an eighty-pound dog that is dangling from a tree and you will get my point.

The velcro fasteners at the center top and front of the packs that I use hold the panniers quite well, making brush straps unnecessary.

Three Different Kinds of Fasteners
Top: Double "D" rings (not all ends are "finished"). *Center:* Fastex or quick-release buckle. *Bottom:* Ladder buckle (most ends are "melted" when cut to keep end from unraveling).

Fastener	To Fasten	To Release
Double "D" ring	Loose end is threaded through D-rings	Loose end is unthreaded from D-rings
Quick-release buckle	Snap "together"	Squeeze to release
Ladder buckle	Loose end is threaded through buckle	Loose end is unthreaded from ladder buckle

A pack secured with brush straps.

The pad is correctly placed on this Dalmation photographed by Ed Scott. Note placement of the three straps. *Courtesy Wenaha Dog Packs.*

COLOR

Another option is color. A bright color is easy to see. Black-topped packs get hot in the sun. Earth-tone packs match the forest. White will never stay clean. Blue matches the sky. Some people love red. Newer, more expensive brands are being manufactured in hot pink and other "neon" colors that can be seen anywhere. I have several different colors, selected according to size for easy identification. My medium packs are green; my large ones are red. You may prefer to buy a pack that matches your dog, but sometimes you have to buy the only color that fits. If it doesn't fit right, don't buy it and don't use it no matter what color it is!

FITTING AND PLACEMENT OF THE PACK

Whether you are using a one- or two-piece pack, it is extremely important that the pack is placed properly on your dog. The pack

This is how a pack should fit a medium-sized dog.

This pack is too small for the dog.

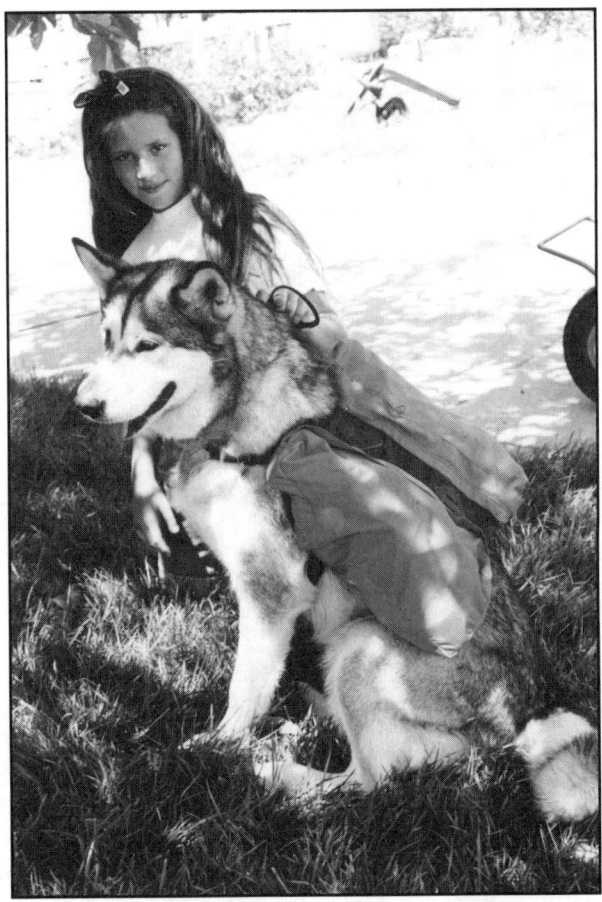

(pad) should be snug, but not tight.

If you are using a one-piece pack, fit the pack to the dog PRIOR to filling it. If you are using a two-piece pack, fit the pad first. Then place the evenly-filled packs over your dog's shoulders. It is similar in placement to placing a saddle on a horse's back. The weight should ride over your dog's shoulders, not on his back. The panniers should hang just to or slightly below the dog's chest at his elbows. At the top, the yoke should be wide enough for the dog's back, but not so wide that the top of the panniers hang down on the sides. The straps should fit in the correct position (see illustration on next page).

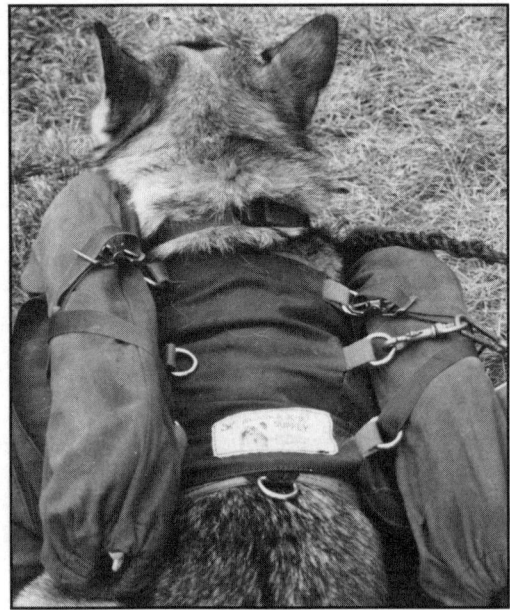

"D" ring at back, this pack is wide enough for a Malamute.

Choosing a Pack   19

Features of a well-constructed pack.

The velcro tabs on a two-piece pack go toward the front, or leading edge, of the pack. These tabs will keep the compartments secured to the pad, especially important when your dog bashes into something. Double-check that all velcro is secure.

Most packs have a loop or D-ring at the back of the pad or pack. Attach your leash to this D-ring or to your dog's collar.

SAFETY TIP: NEVER pack all of your survival supplies on one dog. You never know if the two of you may be separated. And always carry matches on you.

Checklist for Selecting a Quality Dog Pack

- Constructed of durable, sturdy material
- Designed especially for a dog
- Has easy-to-use fasteners
- Zippers are heavy duty with protective flaps
- Double nylon zippers or double sliders or "pulls"
- Leading edge and bottom of each pouch is reinforced
- Has loops or D-rings for securing gear to the outside and top of the pack
- Fits your dog correctly (the larger your dog, the wider the yoke, or backpiece that joins the two compartments)
- Has reinforced or double seams

A pack must be fitted to the width of your dog's back.

Training and Conditioning

You cannot start training too early, because most of the training starts long before you introduce the pack.

Before your first outing, you and your dog must master some obedience training. The MINIMUM is learning the "Come," "Sit," "Stay" and "Quiet" exercises. The more obedience skills your dog learns, the better he will behave on the trail. Commands like "Back," "Behind Me," "Down," "Easy," "Leave It," Stop," and "Wait" will make your trip much easier.

Train your dog to calmly accept children, other hikers, bikers, and animals before you take him on a real trail. On the trail you must cross logs and fjord streams. Young dogs will need to learn this. At first, some may not cross streams or traverse log bridges. Others will be afraid of heights or boulder fields. Bring them along slowly, introducing them to a new experience as they master the previous one.

The local playground is a fine place to start. In the playground and other areas near home, find things to climb over, under, and through. Either walk across with your dog or cross first and then call the dog from the other side. Take him around other animals and wildlife if possible, and teach him to walk quietly beside you while they pass or come near to him. Parks with bridle paths, a friend's farm, a country road and similar surroundings offer many possibilities for getting the city dog accustomed to unfamiliar livestock.

Some dogs never overcome their fear of certain objects or situations. If your dog obviously doesn't enjoy hiking, or if you will be traveling in terrain which you know terrifies him, he is better left at home.

Starting training early. Seven-week-old Malamute puppy.

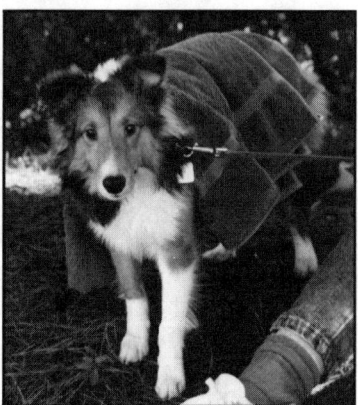

Towel training with six-month-old Sheltie puppy, "Riki," owned by the Julian family.

When your puppy or dog has developed confidence and good manners and can handle almost anything or anyone you encounter on his daily walks with finesse, you can think about introducing a pack. Remember, though, that a puppy should not carry much weight until he is full grown and his muscles are well developed. Then, weight must be introduced gradually with a planned conditioning program.

INTRODUCING THE PACK

The first step in introducing your dog to the backpack is simply to get him to let something be placed on his back. A towel works well for this. At first he may shake, roll, or pull the towel off. Tell him "No" and encourage him to walk with the towel on his back. As soon as your dog leaves the towel in place, give him lots of love and praise. Initially, if the towel stays on for ten seconds or more, your dog is doing great.

Once your dog is large enough to wear a real pack, introduce the pack to the dog. Let him smell it and give him lots of praise. Then very gently place the empty pack on his back. Do not throw the pack on. Place it. The entire time, tell him what a good dog he is. Next, fasten the straps.

Let your dog wear the empty pack around the house or yard for several short periods of time until he learns not to bump into things and tolerates its presence without protesting. Then begin short walks.

I start training with something very light, a box of macaroni and cheese and crumpled up newspapers, for example, in each pack. I use macaroni and cheese because I always have it on hand, and it rattles. Anything that rattles will do. The noise reminds the dog the packs are there, and accustom him to the sound that the packs make when you're hiking in heavy brush. The newspapers are used to fill up the excess room in each pack so that the packs have bulk and sway as the dog walks. Gradually replace the newspapers with more weighty items.

Determining the Proper Weight

The next step is determining how much weight you should use for your training weight, depending upon your dog's size, maturity, and condition. Start light and add weight as you and your dog get in condition. Initially for training use five to ten percent of your dog's weight. Gradually work up to twenty-five percent. Larger breeds (like my Malamutes) often carry up to forty-five or fifty percent of their weight.

Items that work great for weights include small sacks of flour or sugar, canned goods or shoes. For balance, place one of each item in each pack. We pass by a grocery store on our daily walk. Frequently I ask the dogs to carry a few groceries home.

A small or medium size dog, may only be able to carry some water and a portion of her food. A large dog, however, can carry all of her own food and water, plus part, if not all, of your food. Remember, every pound your dog carries is one less pound for you to carry. As a bonus, you can (more than likely you will) change the types of food you take into the back country. That's one advantage of having your dog carry a pack.

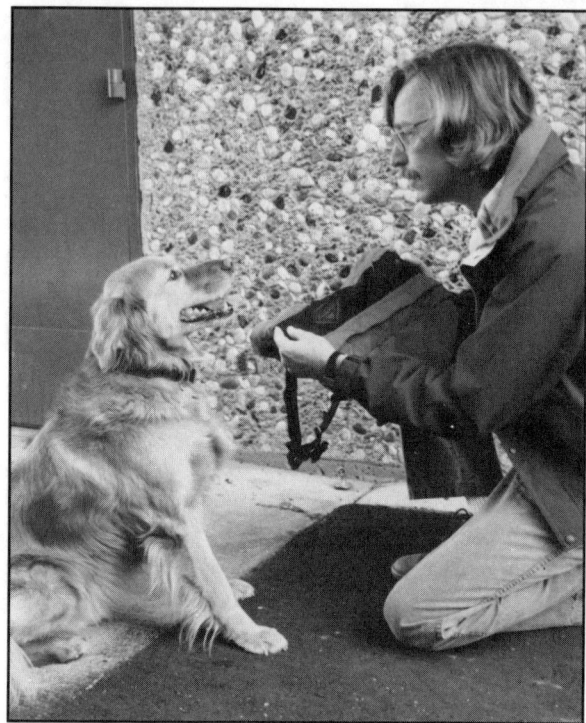

John Pensock introduces a pack to Spenser, a six-year-old Golden Retriever.

Training Walks

Now you are ready to go for your first training walk. You can train on your dog's daily walk. If you don't walk daily, you should walk your dog at least two or three times a week for several weeks before you attempt an overnight trip into the backcountry. Make time for training. You cannot walk or train too much. The minimum distance for these conditioning walks will depend on how far you are planning to backpack (or day hike).

Pack a picnic lunch and carry half of the picnic supplies yourself while your dog carries the other half. If your dog carries her share with no problem, the next time you can add a few more items to her pack. If, for example, you plan to hike three to five miles per day, start your training sessions with walks of at one mile each. Work gradually up to the desired condition. Three to five miles per day is plenty for your first few trips.

If your dog has a problem keeping the pack on, slow down. Whatever you do, don't yell or punish your dog during this introductory outing. A bad experience now may ruin all the good times you could have in the future.

A few short day hikes will build endurance and stamina, and will help you to determine both your own and your dog's condition. Your first trail should be flat and easy. (At times I wish all trails were flat and easy.) Take the elevation and the weather into consideration, too. If you pack twenty pounds on a flat trail it will seem lighter than it does on a steep trail. That same twenty-pound pack will feel even heavier if the weather is hot, or it is raining. The same is true for your dog. Don't increase the weight of the pack by several

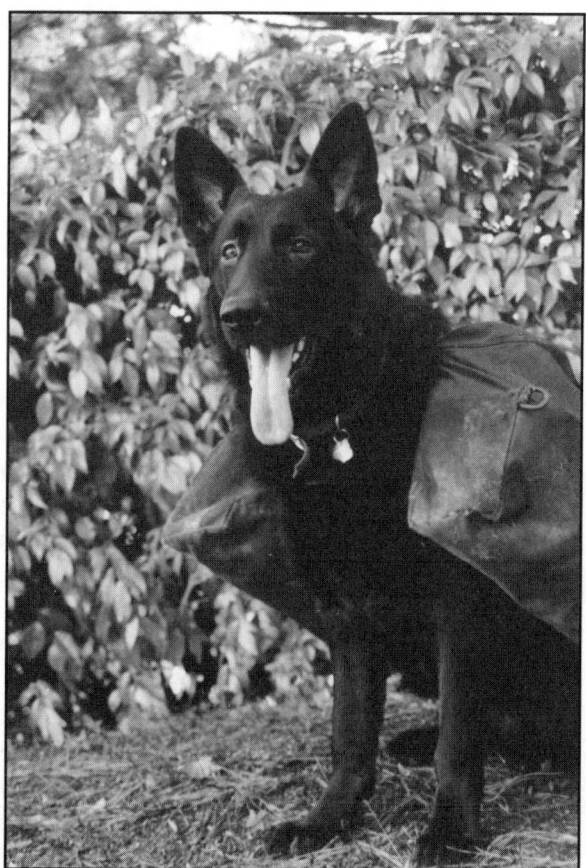

Max, an eight-month-old German Shepherd dog, owned by Kathi and Paul Davenport, is already carrying quite a large pack.

pounds at the same time you first ask your dog to climb a steep, rocky trail. Make only gradual changes. Add a little more weight, or hike a steeper trail, or at a higher elevation or in snow. You can't over-condition.

TEACHING YOUR DOG WHERE TO WALK

There are three places where your dog can walk when you are hiking together: 1) in front of you; 2) beside you; or 3) behind you. Each position has some benefits and some drawbacks.

In Front

This is the most common place where dogs hike. On a narrow, uphill trail, I like to have my dog in front so I can take advantage of his pulling power. (And mine love to pull.)

Pros: You can watch your dog carefully because he is within your vision as you hike. The dog is most comfortable walking in front of you because this is where most dogs are used to walking. If you attach the dog's leash to the padded waistband of your backpack, both of your hands will be free. You can also attach the leash to a strong leather belt so that your whole body handles the force of the dog's pull, which can be helpful for those first uphill miles.

Cons: Your dog will see things in the trail before you do, so you must keep him from bolting after anything that attracts his attention. For example, on a warm day you need to watch for "critters" sunning themselves on the trail. In rocky terrain, darting lizards or chipmunks can distract your dog into bolting first one way and then the other. And if he likes to pull, it is much easier for him to pull you, even when you don't want to be pulled, as when hiking downhill. If your dog walks in front of you, and especially if you are letting your dog pull, attach your leash to the D-ring on the pack. This way the pad (or pack) works a little like a harness.

Beside You

This is the second most frequent place you see dogs hiking. On nice, wide trails I love their company beside me, as long as they don't crowd too close.

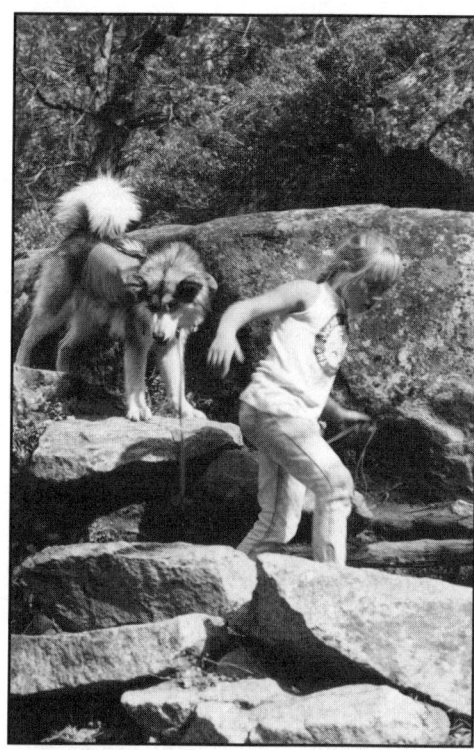

Three Positions for Your Dog

Left: "Stevie" hikes behind Mindy Ivey, Pine Crest Lake, California.

Below: Luke Mason has Kenoshka trained to walk beside him.

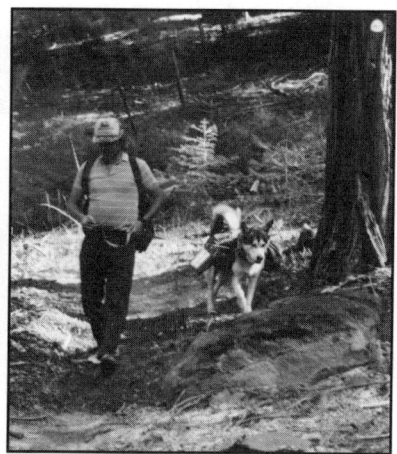

Kenoshka walks in front of Luke.

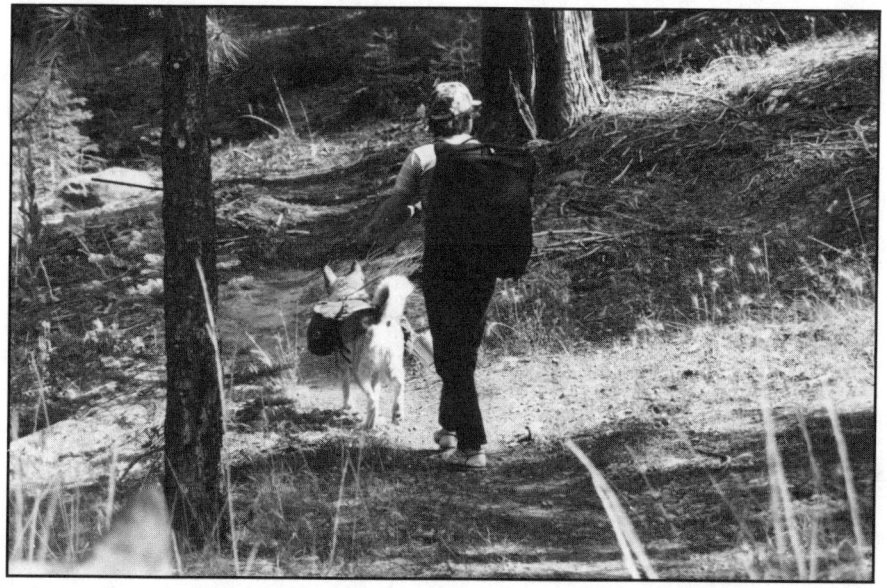

Pros: You can see your dog and can observe him for indications of dehydration or tiredness without breaking stride. His tongue and mouth are the best indicators of when he needs a rest. A dog with a normally pink tongue that has turned blue needs a breather. A foamy mouth on a dog with a normally dry mouth means he needs a drink. It is time for a rest stop. If your dog has already been trained to walk in the heel position he may be more comfortable striding alongside of you.

Cons: Your dog is wearing a pack that may bump into you. This will not work on narrow trails. If the trail is narrow and your dog tries to walk beside you, one or both of you may fall. If your dog walks beside you, attach the leash to either his collar or to the D-ring on his pack.

Behind You

This position is the most infrequent place that dogs are asked to hike. However, on the downhill it's nice to have your dog behind you so he cannot pull you or pass you. (Another advantage for me is that I am able to stop my dog from loving every hiker we meet on the trail.)

Pros: You can more easily control the speed you walk. On narrow trails your dog has no choice but to stay behind you. If your dog has a tendency to pull, you can prevent him from doing so. With a few corrections, he will walk happily behind you.

Cons: You cannot closely watch your dog and so could miss the first signs of any distress. If you want to check on him, you must turn around, which can be uncomfortable when you are wearing a backpack.

I really saw little need for my dogs to walk behind until I made a trip from Whitney Peak back to Whitney Portal. This trail totally changed my mind. It is very much like a narrow, nine-mile-long staircase with uneven steps. There was no way I wanted the dogs in front, pulling me. So, they learned to walk behind, and I have been using this position on steep hills since that time.

On a narrow trail it is easy to train your dog to hike behind you. Hook the leash to her collar, hold the leash in your hand with your arm behind you for the first few steps. You may also use a walking stick to block the way, and keep repeating "Stay behind me." Your dog will quickly pick up on this. Occasionally you may need to swerve in front, blocking her a little to remind her where she is to walk. Do not keep holding your arm behind. You only do that for the first few seconds to cue the dog to the "Behind" position.

When asking your dog to walk behind you, attach the leash to his collar.

As you can see, there are pros and cons for each position. Where your dog walks depends on which direction you are traveling and the condition of the trail. (My dogs enjoy walking in the shade cast by my shadow.) Watch your dog. On really warm days you may notice him moving to sit in your shade when you stop. Make your dog walk where you both feel most comfortable. But remember, you should never allow him to drag you downhill. If your dog pulls, make him walk behind you.

TRAIL MANNERS

From the very beginning of training, observe good trail manners. It is becoming increasingly difficult to find places to hike or backpack with dogs. In some areas a few irresponsible dog owners have ruined opportunities for the many responsible owners. So it is important to leave a good image.

Our trained dogs have been accepted and admired by nearly every hiker we have met in the backcountry. At the trailhead, fellow hikers tend to believe dogs do not belong on the trail. Typically, they change their mind by the end of the hike. It could be that they see how much our dogs love what they are doing; or it could be the time we spend introducing our hiking companions to the dogs as we share the popcorn and snacks that the dogs packed in. More likely it has to do with the way our dogs behave on the trail, or to our conscientious concern for keeping the trail clean, the dogs leashed, and protecting wildlife and other animals. Or perhaps they observe the amount of other people's garbage we pack out, or the delicious change in our backcountry diet due to extra space in our dogpacks. We have even let fellow hikers put their food with ours, on poles with the dogs staked below, a surefire protection from marmot invasions.

There are several ways you can make a good impression while on the trails:

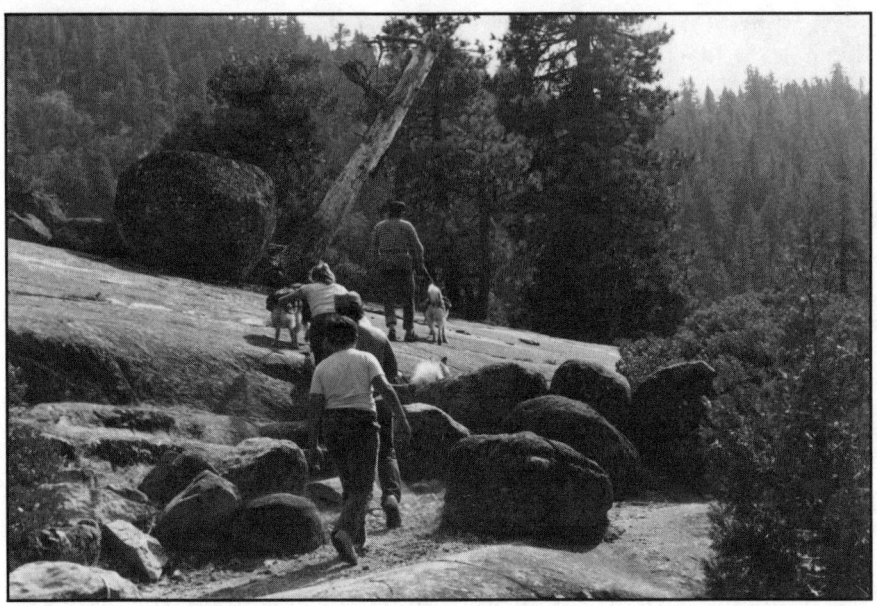

Hikers on the Pine Crest Lake Trail in California.

- Obey the rules. Don't take your dog into areas where dogs are prohibited.
- Keep your dog on leash.
- Wait for other hikers to invite your dog before allowing him to approach them.
- Prevent continuous barking.
- Never hike with an aggressive or uncontrollable dog.
- Move off to the side anytime someone will be passing. (Sometimes we have waited five minutes for a narrow set of switchbacks to clear.)
- Wait until all "down" traffic passes before you start up a narrow trail, or wait at the top for the "up" traffic to clear before you start downhill.
- Smile and say "Hi" to every hiker you pass. If you have time, stop to chat. Educate other hikers.

Training and Conditioning   31

- Respect other animals, (even unleashed dogs), and especially wildlife. Move your dog off of the trail far enough to prevent him from disturbing horses or llamas. Keep him quiet and under control.
- Make your dogs an asset by picking up trash left behind by less responsible backpackers. Mention this to other hikers.
- Make hiking and backpacking an informative, image-building experience.

Your attitude will play a big role in the success of your hikes. Remember not to ask your dog to do too much too soon. If you have any doubt about his physical condition, then he probably isn't ready.

Your training walks should be a special, enjoyable time for both you and the dog. You are together, having fun. It should not be a chore but, rather, something to which you both look forward. Your dog will soon get excited when he sees his pack.

Making your training time fun is important because hiking is fun.

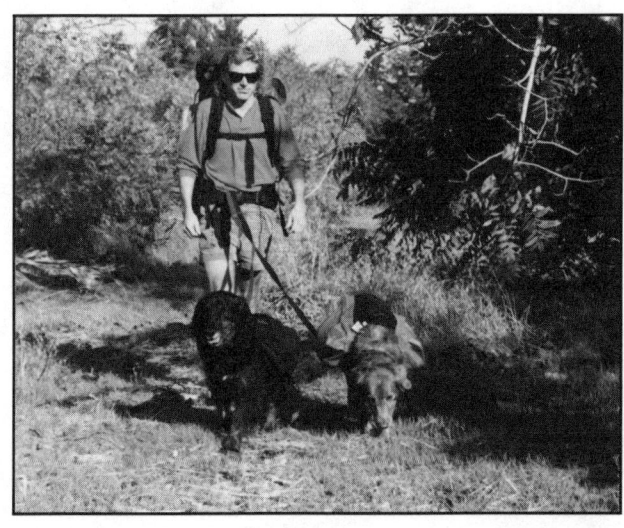

Two well-behaved dogs. If your dogs are well-trained, you can easily handle two, as shown by Mike Hacker with "Bo" on the left, "Clay" on the right.

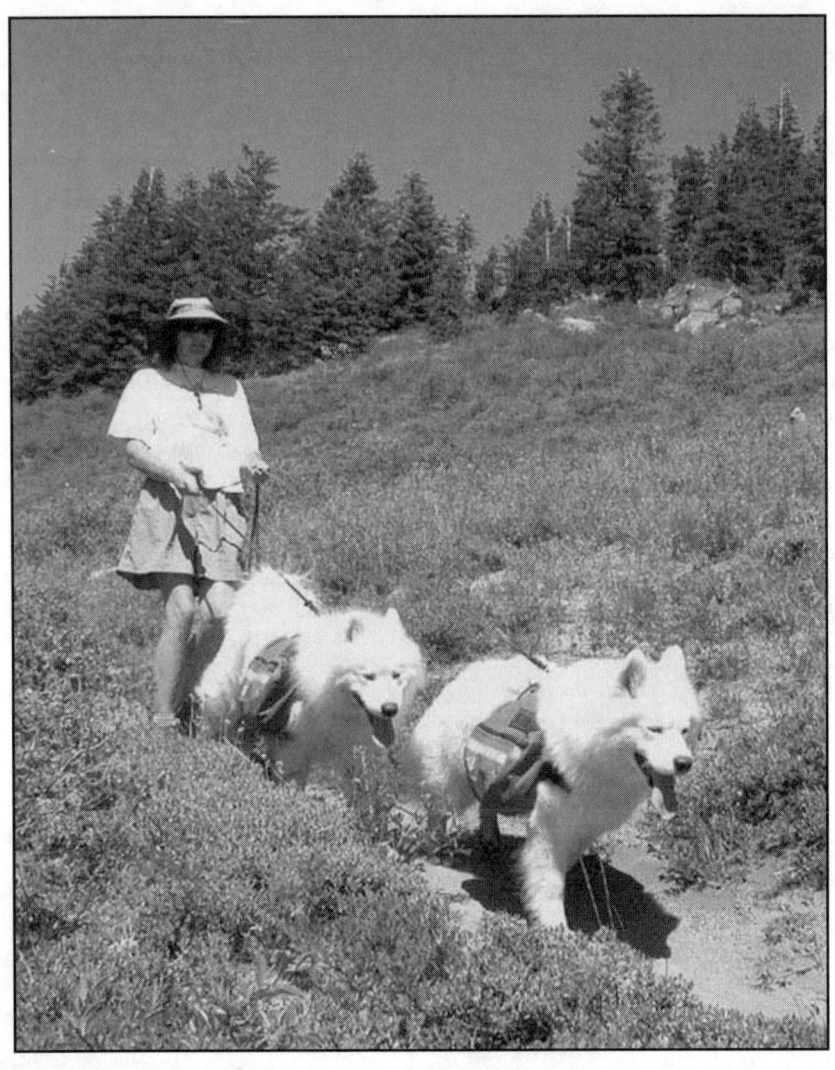

Your first trip might be a day hike on a local trail. Photo © Paul Martin.

Planning Your First Real Trip

The age at which your dog is ready for his first "real" hike depends on many factors, such as where you plan to hike (trail, elevation, expected temperature); how many days you expect to be on the trail, including layovers; the distance you plan to travel (how many miles round trip); how much weight you expect your dog to carry; and the condition of your dog.

If you make plenty of short day hikes, you'll know when the two of you are ready for the "big one." You must be confident of your dog's ability before you depend on him for a real backpacking experience.

It is preferable to wait until your dog is full grown before taking him on a long hike. Most large breeds of dogs are not fully mature until they are at least two years old. Take this into consideration when you hike with any animal under two years of age. However, I have hiked, and still plan on hiking, with six- to eleven-month-old pups. I make extra stops when I have the younger dogs along, and I keep the tone "light" — lots of love and baby talk. It should go without saying that you cannot expect a young pup to work as hard as an adult dog. After your dog's first birthday you can begin to ask her to earn her keep on the trail.

PREPARATIONS

Once you decide your dog is ready to hike with you, it's time to pick the place and time to hike. It's important that you know what the weather will be like when you are on your trip. You don't want to trek across Alaska with a coatless wonder in the middle of

"Who says I'm too young to go backpacking?"

winter. You also don't want to cross Death Valley with any dog in the middle of summer. More practically, for your first trips, pick weather conditions to which your dog is adapted and familiar. Unless he is experienced, in hard condition and excellent health, don't expect him to carry a load in extreme weather conditions of any kind.

FINDING PLACES TO HIKE

How do you find the perfect place to hike? There probably is no "perfect" place, but any place you hike is nearly perfect if you have a good time. I've truly enjoyed just about every mile I've ever hiked. True, some miles were nicer than others. And there were a few trails I don't think I will ever hike again. But, given the opportunity, I would hike most of the trails over and over again.

Word of mouth is one of the best ways to find suitable hiking trails. More than once we've met other hikers who have suggested a great new place we could explore with our dogs. (This is one of those times carrying a pen and paper comes in handy.) But word of mouth isn't the only way to discover new trails. With a bit of research you'll likely uncover a wealth of information about where you can (and can't) hike in your area.

Begin with a visit to your public library, outdoor store or local bookstore. Ask for help to find books on hiking trails in your area. Many of these books, pamphlets or fliers have more information than you will ever need. For example, a pamphlet I found on The Bizz Johnson Trail (an historical trail that runs between Susanville and Westwood in Northern California) told us that the trail is bordered by private property, Bureau of Land Management (BLM) land and National Forest, and is less than 30 miles long.

We also found a series of books on the Pacific Crest Trail (PCT), which runs from Mexico to Canada. The book on the section of trail I was interested in listed the different government agencies along the way, the exact mileage between points, recommended camp sites, locations of surface water, TOPO maps and U. S. Post offices where you could ship your supplies.

A Guide to Our Federal Lands, published by the National Geographic Society, Washington, DC 20036, lists many addresses where you can write for information about federally owned land.

Dogs are prohibited on the trails of most National Parks, but there are exceptions. They are permitted on most, but not all, National Forest trails. The only way to be sure is to contact your local or state parks departments, BLM office or National Forest headquarters for more information on hiking trails in your area. They can tell you exactly where you can and cannot take your dogs. You also need to learn which trails cross from one jurisdiction into another or you could find yourself ten miles into the wilderness on the way to a particular destination when you come across a "No Dogs" sign as the trail leaves one land management area and enters another.

When you are exploring information on local trails, check out the following.

Historical and Jogging Trails

Some of these trails can be rather short and only suitable for day hiking; other trails are much longer. Many parks have jogging trails. A jogging trail near a lake may be the perfect place for a picnic.

If you are like me, many times you don't have the time to go away for the weekend, yet I still want to get out with my dogs and our friends. We often load our dogs' packs with a picnic lunch, go for a short walk (typically we hike five miles to a nice lunch spot), stop and have a picnic lunch. We rest and visit for an hour or so, then walk back to our car. We are usually home by 4 p.m. During a day hike we can go many more miles than when we are backpacking because we carry less weight.

City, State and County Parks

More and more parks are setting up dog areas and opening up trails for hiking with dogs. Let your fingers do the walking and call the park office to verify that dogs are welcome in the park or on the trail. Cross country hiking with your dog in open space can be great fun. After hiking in any grassland, be sure to check for ticks.

Fire Roads and Jeep Trails

Other options in your area might include fire trails, fire roads, logging roads, old railroad beds, jeep trails or dirt roads. There are some definite benefits to hiking on wide trails. For one, if there is a tick problem, walking in the middle of the trail will reduce your chances of ticks getting on you or your dog.

Your trail may be a dirt road, but not all dirt roads are ugly. Open your mind and enjoy each experience. There are many breathtaking sites on logging roads. Another advantage when hiking on wide trails is that several people can walk side by side and chat with each other. (Just be sure your dogs like each other before you head out.)

BLM Lands

The BLM has many small roadside campgrounds with access to adjacent public land. The use fee is minimal and the campgrounds have few improvements, if any. BLM land is usually leased by ranchers for grazing, so watch for livestock.

National Forests

National Forests are large pieces of federal land. It is easy to collect information about them. Your local phone book should have all the phone numbers for the local ranger stations. National Forests are open to the public, and dogs are always welcome. (Note, this is National Forest land, not National Wilderness areas.)

Be sure to let the local ranger station know you are hiking, how long you'll be there, and where you plan to camp. Know the fire danger and carry all permits. There are times when the forests are closed due to extremely dry weather and high fire danger. These closure signs are for your protection as well as the forest's, so please honor them.

Private Property

Do not trespass on private property. Respect the land owner's wishes. Many people will permit you to hike on their land as long as you ask FIRST. Always get and carry written permission when

Casey, a black lab owned by Phil and Laura Hutcherson in the John Muir Wilderness of the Sierra National Forest.

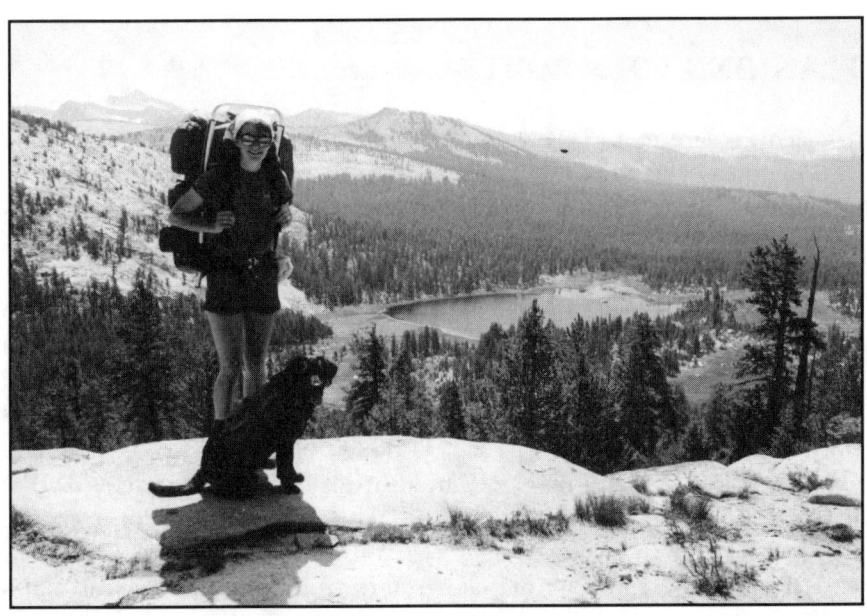

hiking on private property. If the land owner refuses to let you cross her property, find someplace else to hike.

National Parks and Monuments

For the most part, dogs and other pets are not welcome on the trails in National Parks or National Monuments. Exceptions to this rule apply only if you are blind and have a seeing eye dog, if you are searching for a missing person with a trained search-and-rescue dog, or if you are handicapped with a specially trained companion dog. (In California the Companion Dog program is a program where dogs are trained to perform special skills for people with special requirements.)

As you can see, you may have to search a little to find places to hike with your dog. To be honest, where we live in Northern California, most established areas do not permit dogs. But the places that we have been permitted to hike have been outstanding! There have been times we hiked the same piece of trail in the spring (complete with snow) and then again late in the summer. It was hard to believe it was the same trail. There is nothing wrong with spending a lot of time hiking in one area.

PLANNING YOUR ROUTE

Topographical (TOPO) maps make it easier to plan your hike. TOPO maps tell you the grade (steepness of your climb) if any. They also show terrain detail (hilly or flat), surface water (lakes and streams), and the boundaries of private land, national forests and national parks.

TOPO maps can be purchased at many local sporting goods stores and map stores, and from regional United States Geological Survey (USGS) offices that offer over-the-counter map sales of local areas. If there isn't a regional USGS office near you, write USGS Map Sales, Box 25286, Denver, CO 80225 or call 303-236-7477. The Denver office is the only USGS mail order office that carries TOPO maps for all regions in the United States. USGS is a part of the Department of Interior.

If you are planning a trip several days in length, use your maps to figure out how far you want to hike each day and determine

TOPO maps make it easier to plan your hike.

where you will camp. Sometimes it is much nicer to stay on the windy (breezy) side of a hill than to stay in a meadow with the mosquitoes. Also make a mental note of the daily elevation change. Think of every 1,000 feet of climb as hiking a minimum of one mile further.

GIVE YOUR DOG A PREVENTATIVE HEALTH CHECKUP

You've got your maps. You've decided on the trail. It's four weeks before you leave. If your dog hasn't had a recent physical examination, now is the time. If you live in or plan to hike in an area where heartworms are found, have a blood test done to make sure the dog is clear of these parasites and ask you veterinarian about putting the dog on a heartworm preventative. These deadly parasites are spread through mosquito bites and are present in most areas of the country. The mature worms lodge in the dog's heart, interfering with blood flow. Treatment is difficult and expensive and the prognosis for untreated dogs is eventual death.

Four weeks before your trip is also the time to get your dog's first Lyme disease vaccination. Three weeks later (one week before you leave) he will need his second Lyme disease booster shot. Lyme disease, spread by ticks, is also a serious disease communicable to both dogs and humans. It pays to be protected before you go on the trail.

While at your veterinarian's office, ask for a copy of your dog's vaccination record. Be sure all vaccinations, including rabies, are current. I carry a copy of each dog's vaccinations with me wherever we go. Having these records is necessary if you must board your dog. On one trip we had car trouble on the way home and had to spend the night in a strange town while our car was being repaired. If our dogs couldn't have stayed in the motel with us, we would have had to board them.

If you must board your dog when traveling, check with a local veterinarian to find the best places. If you have the dog's vaccination records with you, you will be more likely to find a kennel.

Feet and Nails

If your dog gets plenty of exercise, her nails should be worn down. If not, the nails must be trimmed because excessively long nails will make your dog's feet hurt. Be sure your dog has short to medium nails. If you need to trim the nails, have them trimmed AT LEAST one week before the scheduled start of your hike. Trimming the nails just before you leave on a trip can make your dog's feet tender. Ask your veterinarian to show you how to trim the nails.

Nails should be short to medium.

Using quality clippers or a grinder is a must. On dogs with very long nails, trim a little, then wait three or four days and trim a little more. Repeat trimming and waiting until the nail is the correct length. Removing only a little of the nail each time will allow the quick (the part of the nail with the nerve and blood supply) to recede. This way you will not hurt the dog or make a nail bleed. It also is easier on the dog because there are no drastic changes to its feet. Do not make the nail too short. Nails that are too short make it difficult for your dog to get enough traction and he may slip and slide on smooth surfaces. A dog with the proper length of nail has a much easier time walking, and she won't experience sore feet. A dog with sore feet will look as if he is "walking on eggs," and will carefully place her foot for each step. However, do not confuse sore feet with tender pads.

Pads

Your dog needs to have tough pads. If he lives and walks only on soft grass, he might have a problem hiking on hard (and often sharp) rocks. Most trails are very firm and hard. A dog's pads should be rough and look like fine sandpaper. Worn down pads are smooth and may have little "dots" on them. The dots are nerve endings and the ends of the capillaries (the blood supply to the pad).

There are many products you can purchase to toughen pads. These products are brushed onto the dog's feet. The chemicals used basically "pickle" the pad. Be careful when putting these substances on your dog's feet. Most are toxic if used in large amounts. One home remedy that works well to toughen pads is tannic acid. To

These pads are getting a little thin (worn pads).

make a tannic acid solution, place a tea bag in a small amount of water (⅛ to ¼ cup). Allow the tea to steep until it is very strong. After the tea is cooled, soak each foot for three to five minutes. This should keep the pad tough for several days. If needed, you can make this solution when you are on the trail.

GETTING PERMITS AND PERMISSIONS

Maps purchased. Trail set. Vaccinations complete. If you haven't already done so, now is the time to secure your wilderness permits and written permissions to cross any private property. (In some areas you may need to write ahead of time to reserve a wilderness permit.) Be sure to carry all permits and vaccination records with you when you are hiking.

If you have to acquire a wilderness permit, they are obtained by contacting the agency that administers the land: the Bureau of Land Management (BLM) office; the Forest Service office, etc. Go to the office nearest the land you wish to hike.

Sometimes you can pick up the permit at the trailhead. The cost, if any, depends upon the agency involved. Fines for not having permits are always substantial.

When you get your wilderness permit, also pick up a campfire permit. This is required any time you camp outside posted public campgrounds. It is required even if you are staying on private property.

You will be told what the current fire hazard status is when you pick up your permit, and what restrictions, if any, are in effect. Read the permit for additional details on fire stages and their restrictions, and always abide by them.

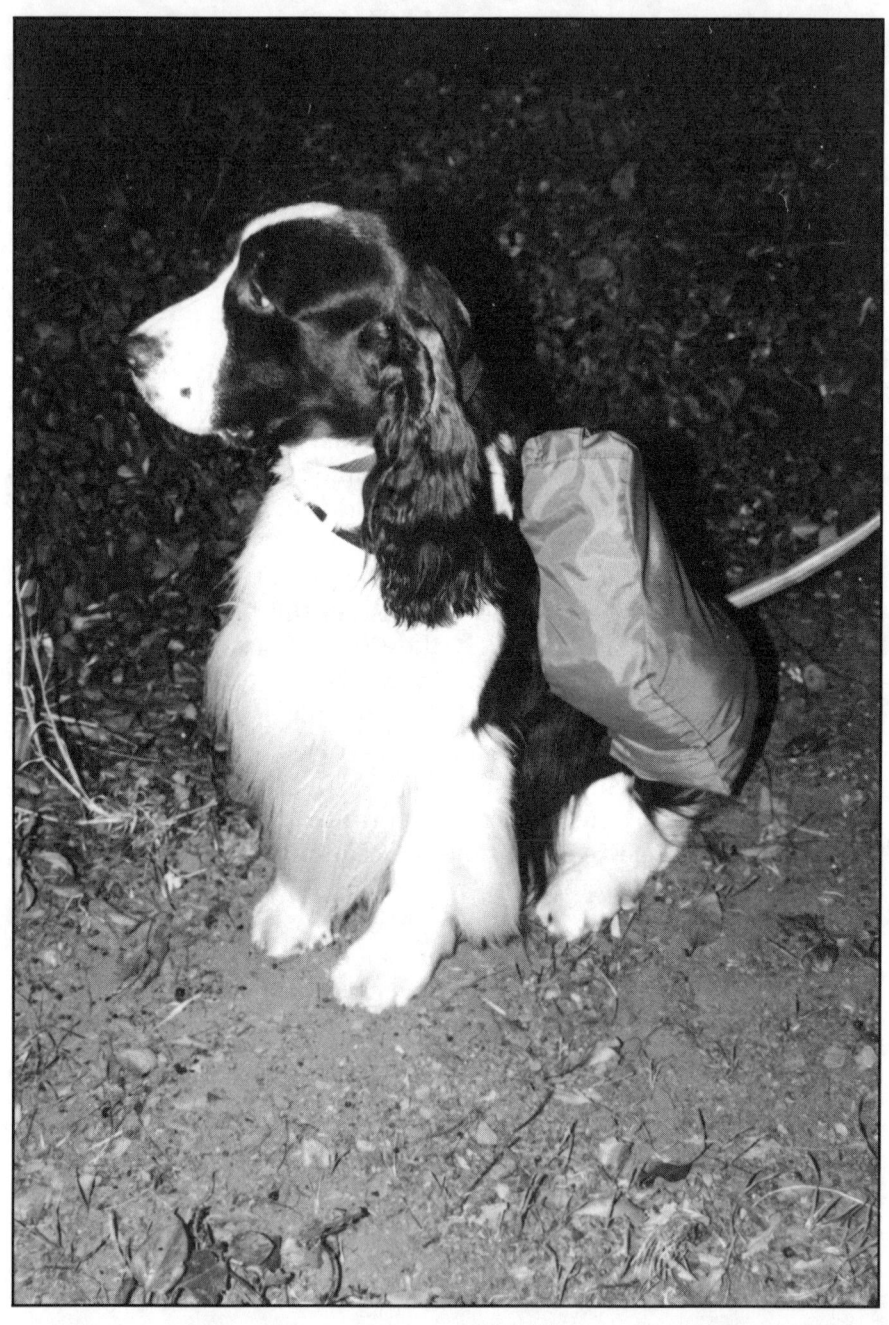

"Skipper," Classic's Forty-Knots, owned by Dale Nakashima and Mona Nichols, proves that small dogs can pack, too.

Planning Meals for You and Your Dog

PREPARING DOG MEALS

Pack each "dog meal" in a separate plastic bag or seal-a-meal container. (If I have three dogs that are all eating the same food, I pack meals for all three in one bag.) Use a magic marker to label the bag if you need to identify the contents. Free samples from dog food manufacturers are very handy when backpacking.

I feed my dogs twice a day — a light meal in the morning and a second meal at the end of the day. When hiking I feed puppy food to all the dogs because they need the extra protein and calories, and because their stools ("landmines") are usually smaller and easier to clean up or move off the trail.

On day hikes, I take snacks for the dogs. On overnight trips I do not take extra snacks. I haven't found it necessary to supplement a quality puppy food. However, I do feed the cooled leftovers from my own meals to my dogs. I put their kibble in the pan and stir in the leftovers. The dogs think I cooked something special just for them.

PLANNING MEALS FOR PEOPLE

The next step is to plan your meals. When you hike with dogs you often have space for "gourmet" foods as well as regular prepackaged or backpacking food items. For example, how does a small canned ham with freeze-dried hash browns and dried or canned vegetables sound? Or consider tuna and noodles, chicken and dumplings, canned beef stew or popcorn? You wouldn't normally take these foods on backpacking trips because you wouldn't have room for them, but your dog's packing ability opens up many new possibilities.

Plan balanced people meals. This is one time you can get away with eating high calorie foods. The colder the weather or more strenuous the hike, the more calories your body needs.

Another thing to think about when planning meals is the size, weight and shape of your food containers. If you plan to serve canned vegetables, take two identical cans. You may use both cans in one meal or have one each for two different meals. Carrying two cans will help make packing, and balancing the packs, easier.

Be sure everything going into the dog's pack is packaged heavy duty. Even unprotected soft drink and beer cans break or puncture easily if not properly packed. If possible, use the heavier freezer-strength plastic bags instead of lightweight ones. You would be surprised to see the holes worn in regular plastic bags at the end

Prepare dog food before trip.

of five or ten miles because the items rub together or against the side of the pack.

A MATRIX FOR MEALS

Meal planning is easy using the simple, two-part matrix illustrated. The first section is for people meals and the second is for dog meals. Fill in the matrix from the first day you will be on the trail through the last. And ALWAYS TAKE EXTRA FOOD.

I ALWAYS hike with extra dog and people food — just in case we're delayed for any reason.

Here are a few ideas for meals:

Breakfast
Instant cereal with dried fruit. Soak fruit overnight in a zip-lock bag.
Pancakes and syrup
Real eggs. Pack eggs in a special plastic egg carrier available at camping goods stores.
English muffins
Rice cakes with preserves
"Gorp" or trail mix

Lunch
Summer sausage or salami (the kind you do not refrigerate)
Canned lunch meat, lunch spreads or lunchmeat spreads
Canned regular or smoked oysters or canned clams (pour leftover oil on dog's food — mine LOVE it!)
Squirt cheese. Cheese in a can that does not need to be refrigerated. Do not take this snow camping. The cheese gets too cold and will not come out of the container.
"Lunchables." These nifty little packages contain crackers, cheese, lunch meat, mustard or mayonnaise and a napkin. These hold up quite well in a dog pack and are great for day hikes or the first day on the trail.

MATRIX FOR MEAL PLANNING

MEAL→ DAY↓	PEOPLE			DOGS	
	B	L	D	AM	PM
FRI 3/4	eat out	munchies lunchables	Roast Chicken mashed potatoes	Eat @ trail head on before we leave home	✗
SAT 3/5	eggs coffee	munchies	freeze dried beef stew	✓	✓
SUN 3/6	English muffin	lunch spread trailmix	fried Spam potatoes	✓	✓
MON 3/7	Pancakes Tea	smoked oysters crackers wine	Chicken-n-dumplins	✓	✓
TUES 3/8	hot cereal	munchies	EAT OUT	✓	(leave) meal in car or eat at home
TOTAL	4 breakfasts	5 lunches	4 dinners	carry 8 dog meals plus extra dog food 4 AM	4 PM

Dinner

The sky's the limit! Use your imagination. You can adapt many of your favorite dishes by using canned or dried ingredients in place of fresh.

Snacks and Desserts

The stuff that can really making hiking with dogs pay off.

Instant pudding

Jiffy-Pop popcorn or popcorn and salt in oil. (It's easiest to use the popcorn that has its own container to pop it in.)

Fresh fruit, such as apples and oranges. Any firm fruit, but these need to be packed in a container, or your apples will be applesauce when you get to camp.

Cookies. (In a box, of course.)

Don't take only heavy items. But it's nice to be able to eat something besides the same old backpacking food every time you hike.

Charlene's Favorite Recipes

ROASTED CHICKEN

Prepare ahead of time a parboiled or microwaved chicken and place in a coffee can. Place chicken and can in the freezer. Freeze hard. Keep frozen until you leave. Place bicycle water bottle of wine next to can of frozen chicken. Using a towel for insulation, wrap both together. Place in dog's pack. The chicken will be thawed in time to cook it for dinner your first night out.

To cook, roast over an open fire and baste with wine. I discard the bones by burning them in the fire. (Make sure the dogs don't get the bones!)

Note: If there is leftover meat, put meat and bones in a pan. Add dried veggies, cover with water, simmer and enjoy "chicken soup" for breakfast. Add a beaten egg and have "egg drop soup." Yum!

Charlene's Favorite Recipes

CHICKEN AND DUMPLINGS

My personal favorite! This basic recipe is easy to make. You can alter it a little each time you make it by simply changing the vegetable(s) and/or soup mix. Add more veggies or dumplings to feed more people. Serves 2 or 3 people and dogs.

Stock/Soup:
1½ oz. can boneless chicken
1 10½ oz. can cream of chicken, celery or mushroom soup
or: 1 packet dried soup/dip mix (cream of chicken or celery)
or: 3 packets cup-of-soup (cream of chicken or celery)
2 tablespoons dried celery
2 tablespoons dried onion
Dried vegetables (peppers and carrots)
or: freeze-dried backpacking green beans or peas
2 to 3 cups water (altitude and veggies will determine amount)

Dumplings:
1 cup Bisquick or other baking mix
1 tablespoon dried parsley flakes
¼ teaspoon garlic powder
1 teaspoon poultry seasoning
⅓ to ½ cup water

Mix all dry dumpling ingredients together in a resealable bag. (I do this before I leave home.) Pour ⅓ cup water in bag with dumpling mix. Reseal. Gently squeeze bag to mix. Add more water if dumplings are too thick. Set aside.

Put 2 cups water in large pot. Add dried vegetables (the kind that must be soaked for hours, not the freeze-dried backpacking ones). Cover pot and bring water to a boil. Add remaining soup stock ingredients. Stir for 2 or 3 minutes to mix.

Cut corner off bag with dumplings. Squeeze dumplings into pot. Cover pot. Turn down heat, simmer 5 to 10 minutes. Uncover and stir gently, then re-cover and let cook 5 more minutes.

Turn off heat and let stand covered an additional 5 minutes. Serve and enjoy.

WATER FOR YOU AND YOUR DOG

You will use a lot of water on a summer backpacking trip. At one time you could safely drink from running streams in the wilderness, but today most water in the backcountry is unsafe for either you or the dogs without some form of treatment.

Giardia, a form of protozoa or single-celled organism is something all experienced hikers have heard about and do not want to encounter. Highly contagious, these organisms are found in surface water and cause abdominal cramping, diarrhea, and gas that will bother you for weeks. If infected, you must be treated with prescription medication, and then you may have to go through the medication cycle twice. Giardia cause similar symptoms in dogs, especially seriously dehydrating, watery diarrhea that is easily transmitted to other dogs at home, and is life threatening to puppies. Therefore prevent your dog from drinking from streams, ponds, or puddles, too.

If you need a reason to purify your drinking water, Giardia is only one. There are a multitude of living organisms found in water. Add to these organic debris, human pollutants and contaminates.

Water Containers

You can use almost any container for water as long as it is clean, lightweight, and doesn't leak. Suitable containers for carrying water when hiking or backpacking include but are not limited to:

- Bicycle water bottles
- 2-liter soft drink containers. (These do not always fit in dog packs.)
- Heavy plastic containers of mineral water.
- Hiking water bottles.
- Any sturdy container that can hold liquid. I do not recommend glass or any thin container that may get punctured or break. My dogs have punctured unprotected soft drink cans.

Insulating sleeves work well to protect cans and keep the contents cool.

Filtering or Treating Water

After a day on the trail, all the water you carry or use will be either filtered or treated.

Various types of water containers.

My filter takes five minutes or more to filter one gallon of water. Three people with three dogs, usually need at least six gallons of water. Filtering water is the first thing we do when we set up camp. We use the dogs' buckets to haul water to camp, then filter the water into a two-and-one-half gallon collapsible container that we hang and use to refill the smaller water containers. This cuts down on the amount of water we spill when attempting to pour water from one container into another.

Water filters can be purchased at outdoor shops and backpacking stores. Purchase a quality filter. It will be used to purify the water you and your dogs drink as well as the water you use for cooking and clean up. A quality filter may also come in handy at home should there be any interruption of your water supply, or when you travel. Buy a good filter — it's worth it.

The other choices are no treatment (you run the risk of getting ill); and boiling or chemically treating water for your consumption.

Planning Meals for You and Your Dog 53

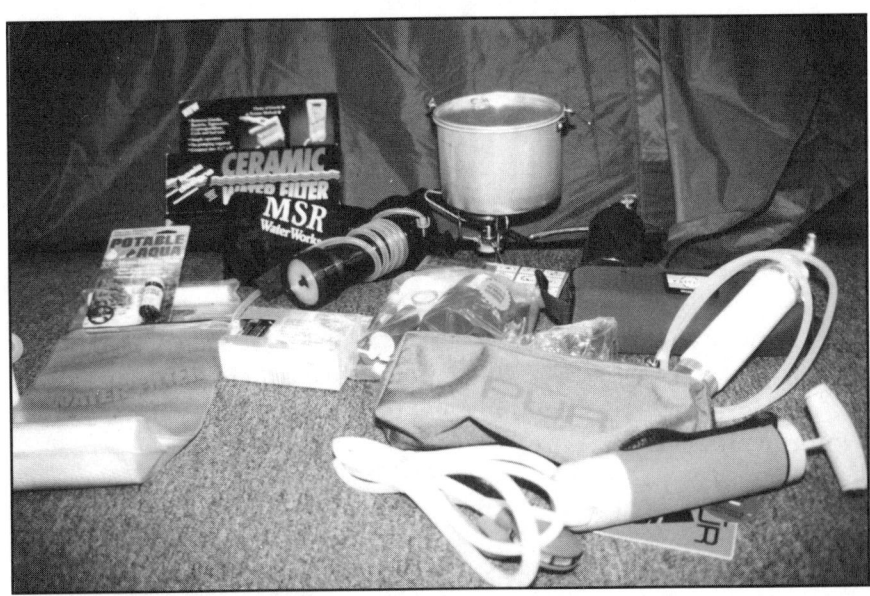

Different types of equipment for purifying water.

Filtered and unfiltered water.

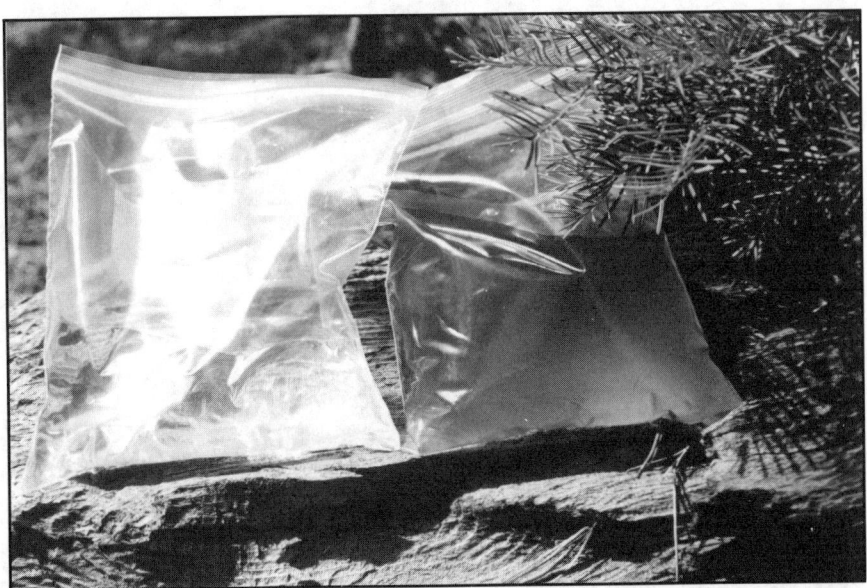

Boiling or chemically treating water doesn't remove the debris in the water; it only kills bacteria and other living organisms. If you choose to chemically treat your water, follow the directions on the container and do not rush the process. Chemical treatment kits are available at sporting goods stores.

If you choose to boil the water, you need to boil it for a full five minutes and then let it cool before using it. Pouring the water through a cloth will remove large pieces of debris, plant matter and sand.

I prefer to drink filtered water. It is clear. A good filter can turn yellow water from a cow pasture into clean, clear, great-tasting water. However, you should always try to find and use the cleanest water available.

Make it a practice to stop and check your dog's pack periodically to be sure that it is balanced and is not rubbing anywhere. Iris is wearing a Wenaha Explorer III.

Packing Up

WHAT TO TAKE

In addition to the "equipment" items listed previously and the "people" gear you normally carry backpacking, be prepared for all your dog's needs and you'll both enjoy the trip more. You still need to pack for yourself, of course. For those of you who have never backpacked overnight into wilderness areas, there are many fine books available at your local library or bookstore that can help you.

Dog Necessities
Regardless of how far you plan to hike, you will always need to pack the following items for your dog:

- Water and a dish. Carry water for both you and your dog.
- First-aid kit with supplies for both you and your dog.
- Dog food and/or snacks.
- Dog sweater or emergency blanket.
- Proof of vaccinations. Some places require proof of rabies vaccination. Without proof you will not be allowed to take your dog.

Overnight Necessities
Many of these items are a must for overnight trips, and will make your day trips more pleasant, too.

- Tie-outs, chain or rope. So you can secure your dog to a rock or tree at mealtime or overnight.
- Bug spray or bug repellent and a new flea collar for your dog.

This is the gear needed for one person and two dogs for two days and one night on the trail.

- Something to use to clean up after your dog. I carry a small hand trowel in a plastic bag. (On overnight trips this is handy for people, too.) This shovel can be in addition to the one you carry if you plan to have a camp fire.
- Meals for your dog, packed in crush-proof, air- or water-tight containers.
- A spray bottle. This is a good way to cool both you and your dog.

Extras

The following items are not "doggie items," but they sure make "roughing it" a little easier.

- A walking stick. Not a must, but mine is worth its weight in gold, many times over!
- A chair or chairs. I have a pair of chairs that fold and roll up. Each chair weighs less than four pounds in its stuff sack. And they tie to the top of the dog pack. They are nice to have at lunchtime on day hikes and wonderful to have in the back country.

A chair, a walking stick, and a basin are nice "extras."

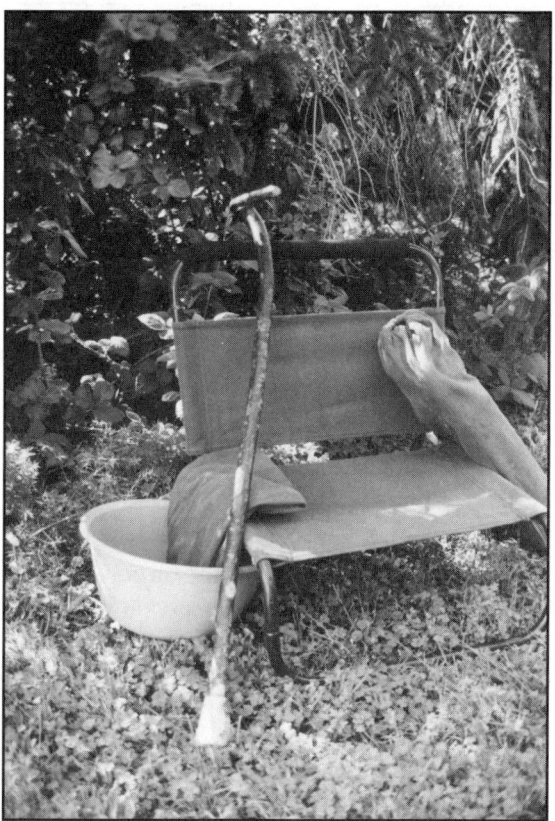

- A collapsible water jug. I use a 2.5-gallon jug. We filter water into it and hang the filled container from a tree. It makes filling individual water containers a breeze. An indispensable overnight item.
- A plastic water basin makes dishwashing easy, and great for washing socks, too. A useful overnight item.

HOW TO PACK THE DOGPACKS

Collect all the items you wish your dog to carry. Put all items in one place, then sort them between the various packs. Never have your dog carry items that can break or that will be damaged if they

First Aid Kit for Dogs

When packing your supplies, be sure to add the following first aid supplies to your first aid kit.

- *An old sock.* This can be used to hold a dressing in place or to keep a leg injury clean.
- *Dog booties* to protect injured pads.
- *Duct tape.* This will keep a dressing in place. It can also be put at the end of a sock to protect an injured pad (makeshift bootie).
- *4-inch square gauze pads.* You should already have some of these in your first aid kit. Bring extras. Your dog will attempt to remove just about anything you use to dress his wound.
- *Cling-type roll bandages,* such as Vet Wrap. These stay on better than do plain gauze rollers. Bring extras for the same reason as your extra gauze pads.
- *Pain reliever.* Aspirin, buffered or baby aspirin, or ascriptin. NOTE: The amount depends on the size of your dog. See your vet for the proper dosage.
- *Steri-strips* or some sort of butterfly closure.
- *Disposable razor.* In case you need to shave hair to expose an injured area.
- *Antiseptic solution* such as Betadine for cleaning cuts and abrasions. Betadine costs a little more but it really works.
- A "leg" from a pair of panty hose will make an *instant muzzle.* Wrap it over the dog's muzzle, cross under his chin, and tie it behind the ears. Do not make it too tight; the dog should be able to breathe but not bite. (Try this at home, before you need it.)
- *Snake bite kit.* The best products currently on the market are kits that use suction to remove the venom, like the Sting-X-Tractor or Sawyer's The Extractor.
- *Mosquito, flea and tick repellents* for both you and the dogs, plus some kind of ointment for insect bites.
- *A tweezer* or small needle-nose pliers to remove porcupine quills or splinters. (Unnoticed porcupine quills on the ground can puncture a dog's pads.)

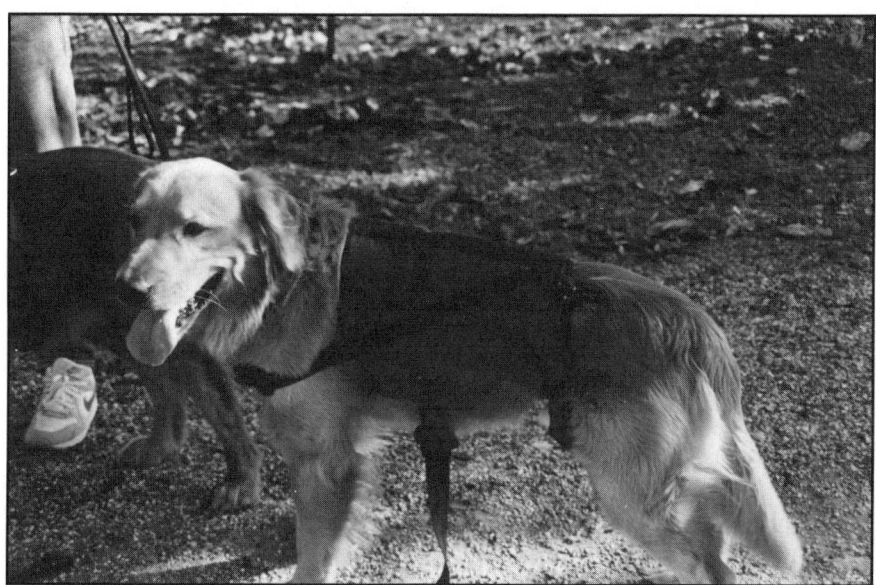

This pad on Beau, owned by Sue Watson, is too far back. The front of the pad must be over the shoulders.

This pack is correctly fitted and placed. Rising Star of Dover owned by Diane Steman.

become wet. NEVER PACK ALL YOUR SURVIVAL SUPPLIES ON THE DOG. Always carry matches in your own pack. In an emergency the two of you might become separated.

Before you start putting items into the pack, fit the pack to the dog. Make sure the breast band and pad are adjusted to focus the weight over the shoulders rather than at mid-back. Secure the loose ends of all straps. Use heavy-duty freezer bags to package the items you want protected from moisture. It's amazing how quickly holes can wear in the thinner plastic bags. Packing items in plastic will protect the contents in case your dog takes an unexpected swim.

Size, Shape and Weight

The items going in the dog's pack must be packed by size, shape and weight. Soft items should be placed on the inside of the pack, next to the dog's side. Make absolutely sure that no sharp or pointy object will poke your dog in the ribs or legs.

The front edge of the pack will take quite a beating, especially on narrow trails. When your dog first starts hiking with a pack, she will bump every tree and rock. After a short distance as she becomes accustomed to the extra width she should no longer bash into things. Canned goods fit nicely in the front edge of the pack. If you are not taking any canned goods, place the packages of dog food here.

Water containers and water dishes should be easy to get to. I pack bicycle water bottles toward the back of each pack so they are protected and easy to reach. If you plan on eating lunch on the trail, pack your lunch where it's easy to remove, also.

Pack each side pack carefully, using lots of padding. Clothing and towels work nicely as padding. Canned fruit juice or box drinks are great on the trail, but both need to be well protected. Wrap a towel around the can or box, then place it against the side of the pack next to the dog. This protects the drink as well as holds the padding next to the dog's side.

Put the heaviest items on the bottom of the pack, and the most easily crushed or the items you will need most frequently should go in the packs last, at the top. If you take crackers, leave them in their box. You will be surprised to see how badly mashed such items become.

Left: All of these items were packed into a dog pack weighing twenty pounds. *Above:* Almost full!

A sweater and lunch go in last.

The full twenty-pound pack.

These packs are uneven in weight. Note how they have shifted. "Einstein," a Great Dane owned by Sharon McCracy and Dan and Marilyn Larkins of Dan-Mar.

Pack Evenly

The weight must be balanced evenly on both sides of the dog. If one side has more bulk or weight, the pack will not ride properly. If the weight is unevenly distributed, one side will hang lower than the other. The sagging pack tends to get in the way of the dog's leg, and if the packs are too unbalanced, they will, of course, fall off.

If your dog tries to walk in circles, the packs are probably off balance. To prevent this, weigh removable packs individually before fastening them to the pad.

To compensate for a little unevenness, you can hang a stainless steel water bucket on the outside of the lighter side. I place the tie-out stakes in one of the stainless steel water buckets that each of my dog's carry.

If you have extra space in the pack, fill the space with a sweater or other soft items. Do not leave space for items to shift as this can wear holes in the containers, including cans and plastic bags. Pack everything with the intent of minimizing the friction and damage to each item. On the return trip, we fill up the empty spaces by packing out other people's litter. We believe in leaving the back country cleaner than when we arrived.

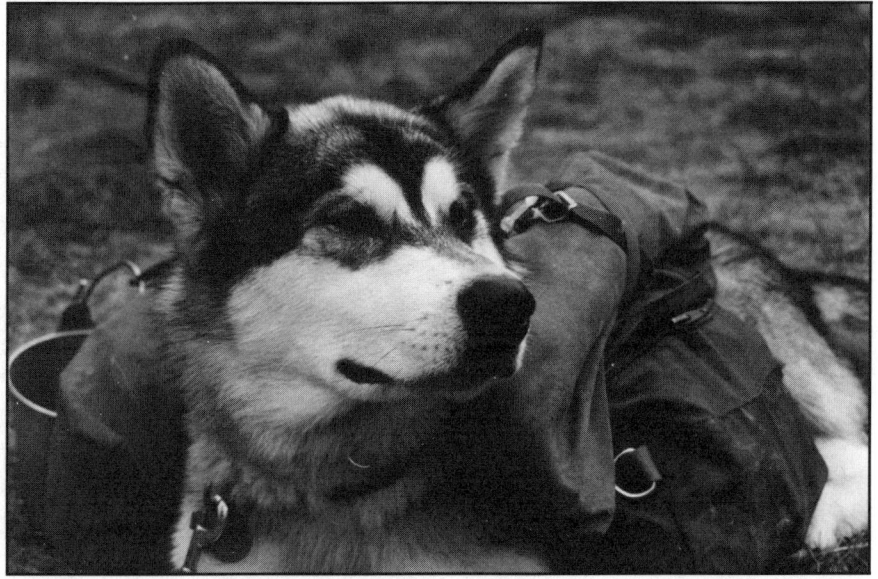

Fully packed and ready to go! Alyeska's Bearly Their WPD, owned by the author.

Northern California Alaskan Malamute Association members Mike Perry, Steve and Charlene LaBelle, and Glen and Vicky Palmer ready for a hike in Lassen National Forest.

On the Trail

The first day of a hike I like to eat breakfast and feed the dogs at home before I leave. Also, I leave the food for the last meal of the trip in the car for the trip home.

Before you leave, make contact with someone to let them know approximately where you are going, and sign in the log at the trail head (if there is one). Log out, and contact the same person when you return. Do this even if it means slipping a note under a door. Remember, if you checked in, always check out.

Any fire restrictions will be posted at the trailhead. Read your permit for details on fire danger stages and the accompanying restrictions. Always carry a trowel or small shovel for preparing and extinguishing campfires.

If you will be hiking in hot weather, get an early start while it is still cool. Plan on temperature changes, and take plenty of extra clothing when hiking in the mountains.

As you walk, learn to watch for your dog's reactions. When he picks up on something, follow his gaze; you will experience many things you normally would miss.

As I stated earlier, it is becoming increasingly difficult to find places to hike or backpack with dogs. Yes, we have the right to take our dogs into the back country, but only where it is legal. We always do our best to leave a good image. Here's how: On narrow trails we move off to the side anytime someone will be passing. Sometimes we've waited five minutes or so for a narrow set of switchbacks to clear. We also wait until all the "down" traffic passes us before we start up a trail, or wait at the top for the "up" traffic to pass. We smile and say "Hi" to every hiker we pass, and often

Keeping Bugs Away

Try these ideas to keep the bugs away from your dogs and yourself:

1. Before the trip, put three tablespoons of Avon Skin So Soft in a quart of warm water and pour it over your just-bathed dog. Rub it in and use a blow dryer to remove the excess water. It keeps the mosquitoes and fleas away.
2. Put a new flea and tick collar on each dog.
3. Spray the dog's legs, chest and belly with a 30-day flea and tick spray that you can get from your vet.
4. Put Avon Skin So Soft bath oil on the inside and outside of the dog's ears.
5. Pour the bath oil full strength on several cotton balls and take them along in a zip-lock bag. (This is not an ad for Avon, but what can I say — it WORKS!)

stop to chat. People find it difficult to believe the frisky dog at the end of my leash carries a pack that weighs 20, 25 or 30-plus pounds.

I even carry business cards when I hike. People who backpack and hike are potentially great dog owners. Any place we go, we enjoy talking about our breed and the pros and cons of backpacking with them. Later I sometimes receive photos of myself and the dogs from people I've met on the trail.

Wherever I hike, I work at making my dogs an asset to the back country. We pick up and pack out trash left behind by irresponsible hikers, and we mention this fact to the people who make comments on how the dogs' packs must be "empty."

If you enjoy backpacking with your dogs and want to see even more areas open to this experience, make hiking and backpacking with your dogs an informative and image-building experience for those you meet on the trail. You may also want to work with parks departments and other organizations to bring about changes in the rules for allowing dogs in our National Parks and promote backpacking with dogs.

And always, everywhere you go, be a responsible dog owner.

REFRESH AND WATER STOPS

Make plenty of "refresh" stops — that is when you stop in the shade for a minute or so and each have a splash of water. A "water stop" is when you pour water into a bowl, let every dog drink its fill, and spend several minutes resting. Plan to stop every sixty to ninety minutes. The hotter the weather, the more frequently you will need to stop and water your dog.

If your dog knows how to drink from a bicycle water bottle, it will make your refresh stops a little easier because you won't need to open the pack and dig out water and a dish. You will still need to make water stops, however.

Teach your dog to drink water from a bottle.

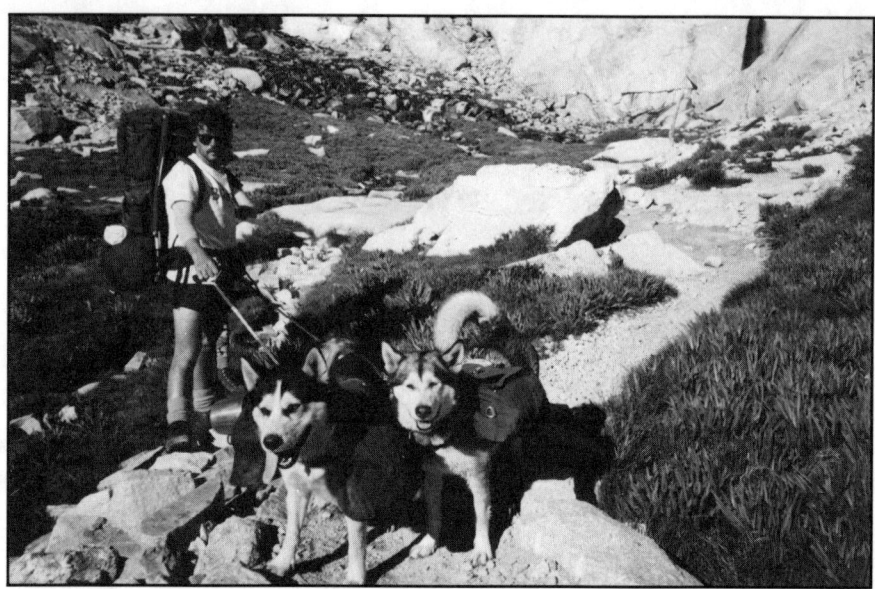

Time for a break!

When hiking with Malamutes carrying heavy packs in 70 degree weather on a gradual grade, we give the dogs between three quarts to one gallon of water for every ten miles we hike.

When the weather is hot, get an early start and consider stopping during mid-day if the heat is extreme. Keep your dog cool. If he stops or lies down in a wet spot on a warm day, don't be alarmed. He is just trying to cool off. Don't rush him. Let him lie in a small stream or puddle while you have a drink of water.

If you are on the trail and your dog seems to have tired or sore feet, find the nearest stream and go wading. The cool water will cool his feet and stop any swelling that may be starting. Wading will feel good on your feet, too.

Watch your dog. If his tongue becomes blue, it's time for a rest stop. This is a sign he is not getting enough oxygen. Don't be upset if his tongue is a little bluer than normal — just take a break.

Also watch for foam at the corners of the lips. Some dogs normally foam at the mouth. If it is normal for your dog to foam at the mouth when he is working or excited, you don't need to worry too much at the first sign of foam. But, when this is not normal for your dog, stop for water and take a breather when you first notice white foam.

AVOIDING DEHYDRATION

Know your dog and do not allow him to become dehydrated. If you have a male who likes to mark everything and he has just passed a large tree without attempting to mark, it may be time for more water. A dog that is drinking enough water will have clear urine. If your dog is not urinating at all while you hike, encourage him to drink more water.

To check for dehydration, grasp about an inch of skin on the dog's neck between two fingers and your thumb. Gently lift the loose skin an inch or two; then release it. If the skin does not immediately return to the normal position, but remains pulled together and standing away from the body, your dog is dehydrating. (Don't pull too hard or grab too much skin.) It is best to experiment with this at home when you know your dog is well and has been drinking adequate amounts of water.

Below, left: This is the way you check for dehydration.
Below, right: If the skin remains up after you let go, the dog is dehydrated and needs to drink more water.

> ### Ice Water Tips for the Hiker
>
> For day hikes, freeze a bottle or two of water to take along. You can use it in several ways:
> - Drink the melted ice and add more water to the block of ice in the water bottle. This will cool it quickly and is very refreshing.
> - Take a soft drink or beer can and wrap it in a towel with a frozen water bottle next to it. You will have a cold drink at lunch.
> - Use ice for treating sprains and many other first aid uses. WARNING: DO NOT GIVE ICE WATER TO AN OVERHEATED DOG!
> - Balance the packs by using several small containers of ice instead of two large ones. Another advantage to the small containers is if one leaks, you won't lose all your water.

HIKING IN EXTREME TEMPERATURES

Expect to be exposed to a wide range of temperatures when hiking. It may be blazing hot during the day and well below freezing at night. If you are a serious backpacker it is best to take survival and first aid training through your local recreation department. Consider carrying first aid booklets for dogs and humans in your pack.

Always be prepared for changing weather conditions. Don't wait until it's too late. If you or your dog gets hot, stop and cool off. If you get cold, put on more clothes, find shelter, or build a fire. Layer your own clothing, or pack extra layers, and take a coat or sweater and booties for small or short-coated dogs when the weather could turn cold.

Hot Weather Problems

Heat Cramps. Cramping of leg and abdominal muscles can occur because of a water and sodium imbalance. Rest in the shade, drink plenty of water, and avoid salt. Gentle stretching or pressure on the affected muscle may be helpful.

On the Trail   71

Wading is a good way to cool off.

Remember to pack items so they stay dry! Sixteen-year-old Thor, owned by Kirt Jorgenson, takes a refreshing swim.

Nine Rules for Hiking with Dogs

Here are nine "rules of thumb" for taking dogs on backcountry trails. The first three rules are perhaps the most important, but abiding by all nine of them will make your trip more pleasurable for both you and the "hiking neighbors" you meet on the trail.

Rule #1:
Clean up after your dog. Never, ever leave "landmines" on the trail!

Rule #2:
Don't let your dog run free, especially around other hikers or where dogs can chase wildlife or livestock.

Rule #3:
Keep your dog quiet, especially at night.

Rule #4:
Don't let your dog bother other hikers in camp or on the trail.

Rule #5:
Give horses, pack animals and other hikers the right-of-way. Many people are frightened of dogs.

Rule #6:
Be nice to the people who believe you should not have the right to backpack with your dog. Don't give them any reason to complain.

Rule #7:
Never forget that your dog depends on you.

Rule #8:
Be a responsible pet owner. Leave the trail and camp spots as clean or cleaner than when you arrived.

Rule #9:
And the most important rule is — ENJOY YOURSELF!

On the Trail 73

Becky Magee filters water as "Mattie" Andalusian Lace of Brigadoon watches.

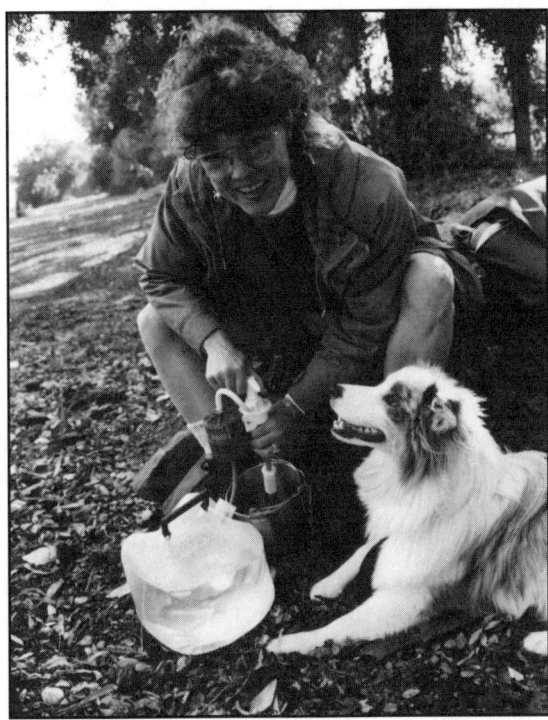

Below, left: The ground was frozen so solid that even our campfire did not thaw it. *Below, right:* Keep your dogs on leash or tethered at all times.

Heat Exhaustion. Weakness, dizziness, and headache occur when the circulatory system is unable to meet the demands of cooling the body. Treatment is much the same as above — get in the shade, drink water, and rest. Dogs can get overheated, too. Rest, give water, and keep them in the shade until recovered.

Heat Stroke. Both dogs and humans are vulnerable to heat stroke. Symptoms are disorientation, confusion, weakness, and fainting. Heat stroke is LIFE THREATENING. Cool the victim as quickly as possible by immersing them in or pouring cool water over them to lower body temperature without chilling. Send for help.

Cold Weather Problems

Hypothermia. Occurs in cool weather, usually in two stages. Shivering in the early stage is followed by drowsiness and difficulty performing tasks. Weakness and poor coordination follows. Hypothermia is also LIFE THREATENING because the body temperature drops to dangerously low levels. Get the patient warm, give warm liquids (no alcohol). In severe cases, get help.

Frost Bite. Occurs when body tissue actually freezes. Treat as for hypothermia and protect the affected body part from further cooling. Do not rub. Do not thaw any frozen tissue. Get help.

The Mountain Bike and Your Dog

Given the growing popularity of mountain bikes, this book would not be complete without a chapter on mountain biking with dogs. I will warn you ahead of time, though, that there are two sides to the issue. I don't wish to use this book to discuss the politics of whether to mountain bike or not to mountain bike in the back country. Those who feel mountain bikes should be allowed say that mountain bikes make it easier and quicker to travel long distances that would take hours on foot. And mountain bikes are a blessing for many people with physical limitations because they can travel to places they previously could not go.

I personally have never backpacked while riding a mountain bike because I don't feel as if I have enough control. But I have hiked with people on mountain bikes, and they did quite well. (I do own mountain bikes and have found them indispensable for running our dogs to condition them.)

If you mountain bike and want to take your dog along, here are some guidelines to follow:

1. Keep your pace comfortable for your dog. Do not go too fast. Don't believe that because you are on a mountain bike that you can go like the wind. (Actually, most mountain bikes are geared at less than 1:1. The pace you go can be rather slow.)
2. Always watch your dog for signs of tiring.
3. Make plenty of refresh and water stops.
4. Be a competent mountain bike rider BEFORE you start hiking with your dog. (Do not take your dog with you when you are learning.)

5. Keep your pace slow and even. Always be in control of the situation. This is a time when owning a dog that responds well to verbal commands is really helpful.
6. When traveling on the trail, it's best to have your dog in front of you. This way you can watch her every move and watch the trail at the same time. Turning around to check your dog can be dangerous.
7. Attach the dog's leash to the gooseneck of your bike. Be sure the leash is attached with a quick-release or deadman's knot. To make a simple quick-release or deadman's knot, get a short piece of rope or cord. The length you need will depend on the size of cord you use, the size of the loop you make and the size of your handlebars. Make a loop at one end of the rope, then attach the leash to the loop. Next, slip the end of the rope through the loop around the gooseneck of your bike. Hold the loose end of rope in (actually it's "under") your hand. Do not secure the rope to the bike. If you fall (and more than likely you will at first), the dog will be freed of your tumble.

PREPARING FOR BIKING

The training, conditioning and preparation is the same for mountain biking as it is for walking. If you plan to ride a mountain bike on your trip, you should do most (if not all) your training and conditioning on the bike. This will also help build competence and communication skills between you and your dog.

A checklist to use before you go mountain biking with your dog follows.

1. Verify that mountain bikes and dogs are permitted on the trails you plan to travel.
2. Check the trail ahead of time to be positive you can handle a dog AND ride your bike at the same time. If the trail is bad, you could end up pushing while your dog is pulling your bike. (I don't see this as much fun for many miles.)
3. Add extra items to your first aid kit such as large gauze squares, antibacterial ointment, and tape to treat abrasions in case you fall.

Hold the rope under your hand.

Attach the leash to your bicycle with a quick-release knot.

4. On the trail, take care of your dog's every need. Check his feet every few miles. Give lots of love and plenty of fresh water. Keep up your verbal contact.
5. When you do fall, don't blame your dog, even if he was the cause.
6. Do all you can to make your time together fun for both you and your dog.

TIP: If there ever was a time you want your dog to understand and obey "Easy," "Stay," "Stop," "Whoa" and "Down," it's when riding a mountain bike on a trail.

Loaded, loaded, loaded . . . and ready to go.

Taking Longer Trips

GETTING READY

Hiking the trails for multiple days, weeks or even months can be a truly rewarding experience. Going on longer trips takes more preparation, but there are some really fine long trails for people who have months to hike. Two trails that come to mind are the historic Appalachian Trail on the East Coast and the Pacific Crest Trail (PCT) on the West Coast. The PCT runs from Canada to the north all the way to Mexico in the south.

Once I have decided I am heading on a trip, I start a journal. The journal goes in my pack during the trip. It may be a bit of extra weight, but I put all my meal plans and other pertinent trip information in that book. The first entry is normally made the day I decide where I will be going. I then spend the time to write down all the things that happen, large and small, while planning and hiking the trail. It makes great reading later, even years later. I may note trail ideas and/or destinations I'm interested in checking out. This takes a bit of homework. Save all of these notes. Some day, a trip you discarded for some reason may be the perfect trip at another time.

The first step for a successful trip is to sit down and figure out where you will go, then plan the route. Determine your start and finish point(s). There are four basic scenarios or types of trails:
1. loop trail, (from "point A" back to "point A" without retracing your steps),
2. a trail that goes out and back on the same trail (from "point A" to "point B" and then back to "point A"),
3. a one way trip from a drop off point to a distant place ("point A" to "point B"), or
4. a combination of the above three options.

If you plan to leave a vehicle at a trailhead for any length of time, you need to notify some local authority. If you go with option 3 (one way), you will also need to arrange transportation at both ends of the trail.

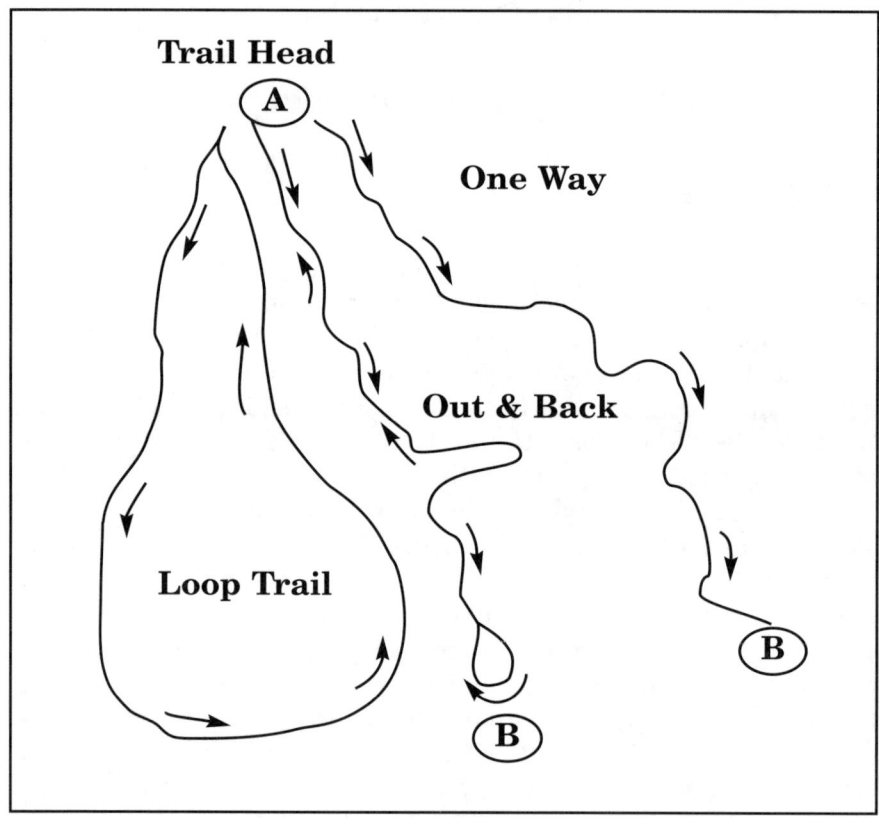

So you know where you are going. Now it's time to plan the daily mileage. Don't plan a trip where you have to run from campsite to campsite. Build some leisure time into your schedule. Determine the actual mileage or linear mileage and then factor in elevation changes and altitude. If the trail goes "up" a thousand feet or "down" a thousand feet, think of this as an additional mile of travel. Also, there could be times you must find your own trail if you want to connect between two trail systems.

If you have a computer, www.topo.com has topographical (or "topo") maps available for purchase online. Some software that is available will plot the entire trip for you with a few clicks of the mouse. I purchased a software program and topo maps for the entire state of California for just under $100, and the packet came with a special waterproof paper to print the maps on.

Plan realistic daily mileage. Plan some days to just relax and soak up the sights, sounds and smells. Plan for bad weather days if traveling long distances in areas that can have show-stopping weather. If at some point you get ahead of schedule, you can just relax and slow down. Enjoy yourself!

MAKE SURE YOU ARE WELCOME

Next, you need to be sure your dog is welcome in all the areas where you must stop. You can through-hike, but if dogs are not allowed on the trail you must plan to get through the area without having to stop or spend the night. Most National Parks will not allow dogs. So if part of the trail traverses through a National Park,

Hikers pose at the halfway point on the Appalachian Trail. Photo courtesy of Paul Martin.

see if there is another route you can take. If there's no other way, trying to hike through at odd hours or even at night will give you less chance of bumping into people who might get upset meeting your dog on the trail with you. Be aware that this is illegal and a ranger may give you a ticket for having a leashed dog on a trail where dogs are not permitted. Some rangers will be understanding if you have been on the trail for days, weeks or months and have no other means of passing through their area. In fact, some rangers will actually go out of their way to help you. On one trip, a ranger gave us and our dogs a ride in the back of his pickup after we arrived at a camp ground and even "made" a campsite for us after we had arrived at a campground only to find that all the sites were full (There were plenty of available sites when I had called ahead.) The gracious rangers went out of their way to find a place for three of us with our dogs to pitch our tent. The space was quite a way from the trail, but running water and a pit toilet were welcome "comforts."

Nevertheless, is still YOUR responsibility to KNOW where you are hiking and to follow the rules.

PERMITS AGAIN

Secure any and all permits, as well as written permission from the property owner(s) if you hike across private property, well in advance. Land owners may forget to mention to a caretaker that you will be passing through. Carrying written permission with you will assist in avoiding conflict. Know the fire danger, and know what you should expect in the way of surface water, and go prepared.

GETTING SET

Plan how much you and your dog can realistically carry day after day. Consumables tend to make up more of the weight in your packs on longer trips. You can take fewer "luxury" items if you will have long stretches between restocking points, so you will want to put more thought into what luxury items you bring with you. For example, you may want to take only the large pot and stove instead of the complete cook kit to trim down a couple ounces.

It helps greatly if you weigh EVERYTHING. The items you take on every overnight trip remain constant: for example, a tent and pad/ground cloth, sleeping bag and pad, stove, dishes, cooking pots, utensils and water containers, jacket, socks, change of clothes, water shoes, toiletry items. In these days of technology, many folks carry cell phones and small electronic devices (to listen to music, weather etc.). But remember, every ounce does count, and you may not have good reception on many of the trails.

Hint: I use a pillowcase to cover my pad. I sleep on 2 pads that are held together by the pillowcase. One pad is an insulating pad and the other is a high-tech air mattress that fills itself when you unroll it.

Plan your consumable supplies and figure how long they will last. You need to plan both people meals and snacks and dog meals. Some food items you may not want to bring because of the fragrance (example: salami or stinky cheese in bear country). Don't forget matches, toilet paper, batteries for the flashlight and fuel for your stove in the consumable department.

People Meals

Plan one set of each balanced/complete for every day on the trail: breakfast, trail snack, lunch, afternoon snack, dinner. Use the matrix in the meal-planning chapter. Remember to add plenty of high energy snacks. Use the food groups and try to balance your meals. Consider taking electrolyte powders or sports drink mixes and a good multi-vitamin.

Dog Meals

Always plan on feeding at the trailhead so you need not carry that first meal. Decide whether your dog will need one or two meals daily. High calorie foods like puppy food or performance diets work best. If you will be switching food, however, be sure to do so well *before* your trip. You don't want to hike with a dog that has diarrhea or an upset stomach. Always carry extra food and plenty of matches! In a real bind, your dog's kibble can sustain human life.

Extra Supplies

Once you have determined the route and made your lists, you can plan the number and location of packages needed to replenish supplies. The need to replenish your supplies is especially necessary on a longer trip because you will not be able to carry everything you need. Consider sending things like a special meal for you and your dog, medications, socks, film, batteries, and other perishables. A charged cell phone battery is a good choice if you plan to carry a cell phone with you. Be sure to include special treats for you and your dog(s). A special item for your dog could be dried liver, a new collar, a fresh herbal flea collar, or a small can of cat food. For you it could be several pairs of new socks, a small bottle of wine or some shampoo, as well as some special food item (like the popcorn that you pop over a fire in its own pan, or chocolate).

In each box put a special meal. This meal could be a "heavy" meal, like a jar of spaghetti sauce, parmesan cheese and a nice pasta. This would be a meal you eat the night you pick up your box, or the following night. Sometimes a burger and fries can be too tempting to pass up since you may be in a town that has a place where you can sit and eat. A quick trip to a local market could net fresh fruit.

After you have decided on how many boxes you need to send and where to send them, clearly address each box to the correct location. Use a sticky note to number the box. Include the date when it is to be shipped on the note. This is essential if you are having a friend or family member drop off or ship packages for you. Time the shipping so the packages arrive in a town on your journey just before you are scheduled to arrive. If you use the U.S. Postal Service, you do not need to know anyone in a town to send yourself packages. Just mail them to yourself in care of General Delivery at the specific town. (I suggest putting a "return to sender" if not picked up by some date well after the time you should have passed through.) Plan on picking up supplies at the post office by Friday or earlier. This way, should you get a day behind schedule, you can still pick up your package on Saturday. The post office is closed on Sundays. You will need identification.

Taking Longer Trips   85

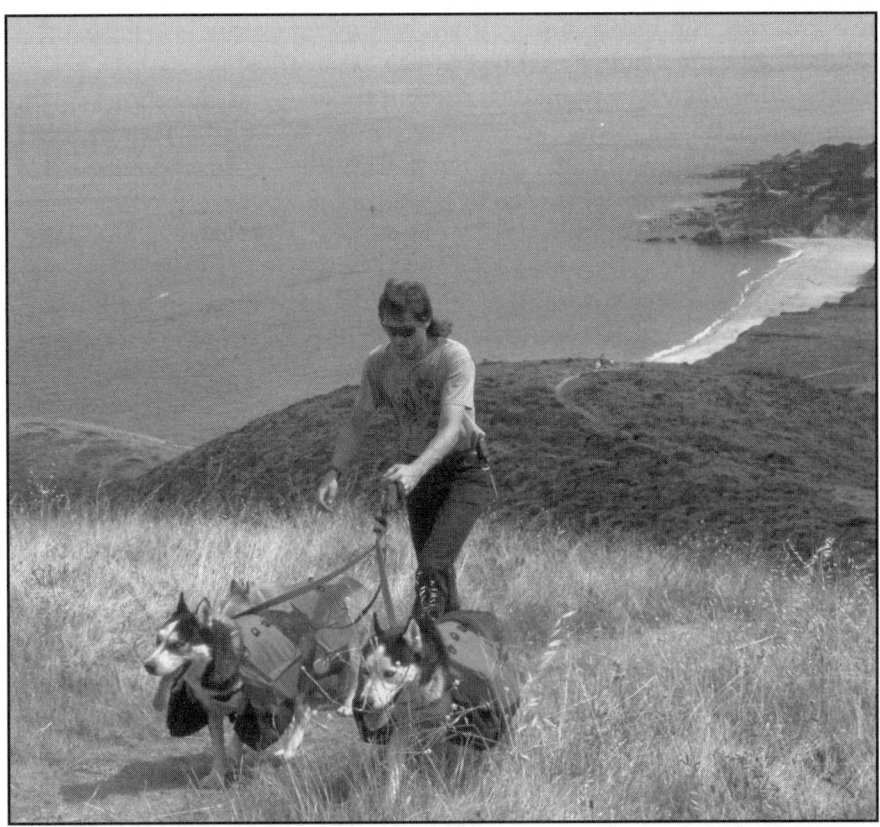

Long treks along the coast are breathtaking. This hiker is walking three dogs in tandem. Photo © Judith Strom.

When visiting the post office you will need to leave your dog secured outside. He can protect your pack if you didn't stash it outside of town.

SUPPORT IS IMPORTANT

It is important that someone knows your route and knows where you are expected by a certain date. If you have friends that can drop supplies along your route where your trail crosses roads, ask them to leave a note on TOP of the package explaining this is a food drop for a hiker. It helps to keep honest people honest and dishonest people from being as tempted. When you call home to check in, you can remind a family member or loved one to drop off a prepackaged, pre-addressed box at the post office.

It is always a good idea to carry a little spending money in the form of cash, maybe a few traveler's checks, and a credit card. Consider your own needs and the possibility of your dog needing veterinary care as well. Medical help for either of you can be expensive and you should plan to have a way to cover the expense if necessary. If you use a credit card on a long trip, make sure you have someone who will be mailing the payments off if you plan to be gone when a bill is due. Your household bills will need to be paid as well. It's no fun trying to charge food and supplies and have your charge card declined. A friend mentioned that some places are no longer taking traveler's checks because of the high rate of counterfeit checks. So, if you get traveler's checks, think about getting a well known "brand."

OTHER ITEMS TO ADD TO YOUR LONG DISTANCE SUPPLIES

Bring a variety of different pain medications (both the type of medications as well as different strengths), allergy medication, topical ointment or wipes to relieve itching from bug bites, and Avon Skin So Soft to ward off mosquitoes. Pack a watch that has *day* and *date* as well as the time. You don't need to wear the watch, but it will help when you are planning a trip into town. Another item might be a small electronic device that minimally you can get the weather on. For cell phones, there are new one-time use batteries available. A paperback book can provide welcome entertainment. For comfort, a small pillow, or even a blow-up traveler's pillow, could be included as gear.

You can always ship unused items back home or ask a postal employee to give them to a needy person or local charity. If you are using and need to send expensive items like rechargeable batteries, compact flash cards/film home, include a pre-addressed envelope complete with postage in the box you ship to pick-up points. This way all you need do is put the items to send home in the envelope and drop it in the slot.

Trash

If you have trash and/or dirty clothes to dispose of, don't leave them in the inside trash can at the post office. Find a dumpster to leave the especially fragrant items.

ARE YOU AND YOUR DOG(S) UP TO IT?

It is important to be honest with yourself when considering if both you and your dog are in condition for a long hike. Take precautions like making sure your dog's feet, nails and pads are in good condition, and that they are used to the heat, cold, humidity, altitude, or other environmental hazards you may encounter. Otherwise, be prepared to take it slow until you both adjust. If you are planning to hike for a week or more, consider the terrain you will be traversing, the amount of weight you are planning to carry day after day, and the amount you want your dog to carry. Are you overestimating your own or your dog's packing ability? Make sure your boots fit comfortably, and that you have pads and medication for your dog's feet as well. This trip should be FUN, not an adventure to endure.

COMMUNICATION IS IMPORTANT

Before you leave, notify friends and family of your intended route and give them a copy of your planned schedule. All contact people should have a copy of the same schedule. Plan and work out a schedule for when you intend to check in. This should be at specific intervals during the trip. Have someone at home marking a map as you go. Have them make date and time notations as you check in at each point.

Never set out on a hike without someone knowing when and where you are going, as well as how or where they might be able to reach you in an emergency. Never hike without letting someone know you got off okay, if you plan to be on the trail for several days or longer. Notify them should ANY plans change. Play it safe, for the sake of both you and your dogs, and your family or friends' peace of mind.

Teach your dog to cross logs as well as to go through water. You might encounter numerous difficult water crossings on a long trip.

DO NOT EXPECT DEVELOPED TRAILS

As you hike more and more regions, you will find that many areas do not have bridges for water crossings. Sometimes a log is used to cross creeks or ravines. Other times wading or swimming is the only way across. If you come to a log crossing and you are with one or more other people, one person should cross the log, and then all the dogs should cross one at a time. Depending on the log and the dogs, you may want to remove the packs, get the dogs safely across, then ferry the packs to the other side. Once the first dog is across, secure him prior to calling the next dog if you are hiking with multiple dogs. Secure each dog before coaxing the next one across. The last person follows, ferrying the packs if necessary. Normally we carry a pack or two from one side to the other and then return for the next pack(s) until all dogs, people, and packs are on the same side. Since my crew normally has packs that are on the heavy side, I can only carry one or two packs at a time.

I don't care for heights and would rather wade through water than walk across a log with my dog on a leash, so I carry a pair of shoes specifically for wading through water. I also wear these in camp to let my feet breathe.

When crossing in shallow, slow-moving water, leave the packs on the dog. If the water is deeper or swift, call the dogs across one at a time and then ferry the packs across. A piece of string can be used to secure each dog's leash to him. Gather the leash into a bundle and tie it to the dog's collar or to the pad while he crosses. You do not want a leash dragging in the water where it could get snagged or endanger your dog. Some leashes have handles that will float. Depending on the crossing and the dog, I may simply remove the leash.

A lot will depend on the water's flow. The volume of water will determine if I carry the dog's packs across first or bring the dogs across first. I would rather make sure the dogs will cross before hauling everything else across. However, it is actually best to bring everything across at the same time because there are times when you cannot go back the way you came. Again, it will depend on what you are crossing: how far, how cold, how deep, and how fast.

If the water is a deep river, you can fashion a raft. Packs can be floated across while you and your dogs swim. I personally will walk the shore until I find a place I can walk across rather than swim.

If the water you are crossing is tidal, you should carry a tide chart for the area. When hiking beaches with cliffs, you do not want to get stuck with nowhere to go as the tide comes in.

In the desert, flash floods can be a real issue. It may not even rain where you are, but if there is a heavy downpour in the mountains above you, a flash flood can result with almost no warning. Do your homework. Know the trail and the weather for the time of your hike. Dark clouds in the mountains could mean flash floods down below. At higher elevations in many areas, it is not uncommon to have a snowstorm in the middle of summer. Layer your clothing, carry extra clothing and a space blanket or Neat Sheet.

PREPARATION AND INGENUITY GO HAND IN HAND

Keeping warm in a tent, as well as protecting your tent floor, is also something to think about. I have been stuck miles from anywhere in a mid-summer snowstorm. If its going to rain or snow, I bring the dogs in the tent with me. I do carry a ground cloth that is trimmed to fit the footprint of my tent. The ground cloth is put down prior to setting up the tent. I have heard from friends how well a Neat Sheet (www.theneatsheet.com) works as a ground

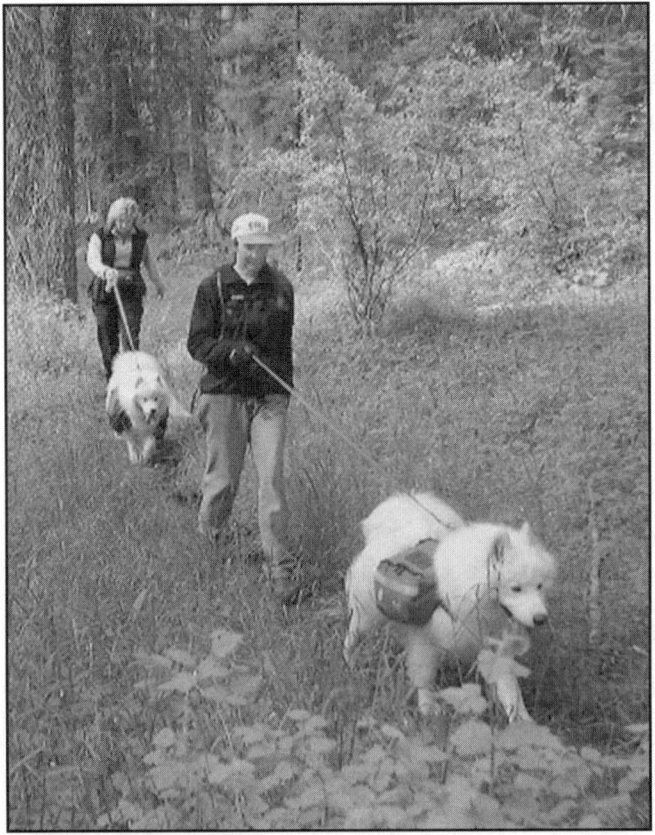

Be prepared for abrupt changes in the weather. Kiba is wearing a Trekker pack made by Wolf Packs, Inc.

cloth. I haven't bought one yet, but I may someday. A Neat Sheet trimmed to fit inside the tent can protect the tent floor from damage from the inside also.

On a cold night, there are little tricks like bringing a heated rock into your tent (place it on some sturdy cloth, like a pair of folded jeans, NOT the tent floor). Choose a large rock that you used as a reflector for your fire–the fire that is either out or mostly out before going to bed. It's no fun getting cold at night.

PROTECT YOUR EQUIPMENT

Some dogs have nails that, no matter how short, make holes in an unprotected tent floor. Here is when dog booties work really well. In a bind, a pair of your own socks will do, but dog booties are so much easier to use if you have them. Booties can be purchased or homemade. You do not need expensive ones. Making them is not that hard, plus you can have a lot of fun with the booties you make.
Booties can be a very important item on long trips because you never know when a dog will bruise a pad on a rock, wear his pads too thin, or get a cut. Using booties routinely on a long and arduous trip will help to prevent injuries. If you don't want your dog to wear them all the time, keep a set or two with you for emergencies. But try the booties on your dog at home first.

SO WHAT ELSE CAN GO WRONG?

Getting sick on the trail happens to a lot of people. If you are not really good about washing your dishes, expect to get the "flu" sometime during your trip. A mild case of food poisoning is very much like the flu. Washing dishes with gravel just does not cut it. You need to use *soap*. There are products like Bio-Suds that are environmentally friendly. Look for products that you can use to wash your dishes, wash your hair, and brush your teeth. Do both you and your dogs a favor: keep a clean camp. Keep your dishes and your dog's dishes clean. Metal dishes can be heated in the fire to sterilize them.

This brings up a safety issue for women and intact female dogs. Women need to know when their menstrual cycle is due, as well as when your bitch will be in heat if hiking with an unspayed female

How to Make Simple Booties

Booties are easy to make if one has access to a sewing machine and a few inexpensive supplies. You can have a lot of fun with the materials. A soft, stretchy material like polar fleece works well. You do not need very much.

Have your dog stand on a ruler or a tape measure and measure the width of his paws. If you make booties for all four feet, measure the front and back feet separately. This measurement plus 1/2-inch will be the width of the bootie.

Cut a piece of the material 10 to 15 inches in length and the width of the dog's foot plus 1/2 inch for the seam. The length can be even longer on really large dogs with really big feet. Fold the cloth in half the long way. Pin the two long sides together.

You will need about one-half yard of sew-on Velcro, or if you can find the stretchy sew-on Velcro, that's even better. Go back to your measurement of the dog's foot plus 1/2 inch. This is the length that you will cut the Velcro (1 piece of hook and 1 piece of fuzz, each the same length as the width of the bootie).

Pin two pieces of the Velcro (hook and fuzz) in the side seam of each bootie, close to the top or open end with the short ends in the seam and the long ends hanging out. The hooks and fuzz should NOT be stuck together. They should be placed back to back.

Stitch close to the edge of the cloth from the open end towards the folded end. Just before getting to the fold, angle the stitches to make a rounded corner.

Flip the cloth over and stitch from the top towards the fold, rounding the corner again as you get to the fold.

Trim off any excess cloth at the bottom corners. For simple hiking booties I do NOT turn the cloth inside out. The stitching stays on the outside. If you want to turn them inside out, you will need to sew the Velcro in with the long ends towards the inside. If I am making booties for use in snow, then I turn the seam to the inside to cut down on places where snow can accumulate.

Fit ONE bootie to the dog before making the other three booties. Wrap the Velcro around the dog's leg and fasten. When tightened, the Velcro should be snug but not tight. If your dog has dewclaws, you need to fit a bit more carefully than a dog without dewclaws. The Velcro holds the bootie on. If it is too tight it will cut off circulation. Don't worry if the bootie slides down or flops around on the dog's foot.

Once the first bootie has been correctly fitted, make the balance of the booties for your entire trip. Let your dog wear the booties around home so that he gets used to them before your trip. Once your dog is accustomed to wearing them, he will forget they are in place. Some campers put booties on their dogs at night so their nails don't tear tent bottoms.

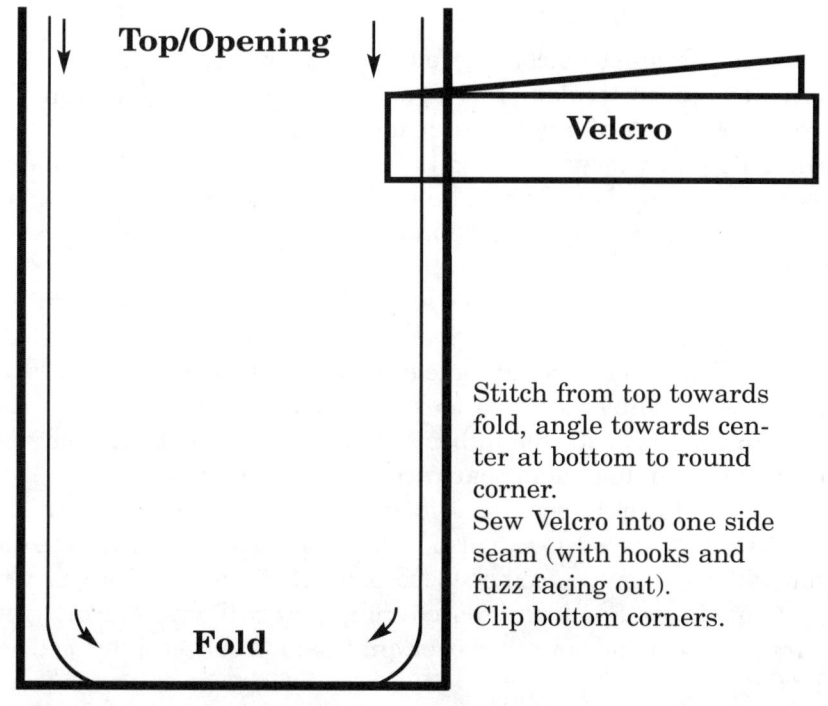

dog. If you are taking a long trip and will be menstruating during your trip, you just might want to pamper yourself and spend a few nights in town with a soft bed with a hot shower. This is not just a comfort issue, but a safety issue because the local wildlife can be attracted to your scent. Then there is the issue of disposal of used sanitary products.

Most female dogs will advertise when they are getting ready to come in heat. Some become escape artists. Others just want to sing all night long. It is no fun hiking with a lovesick male, either. In any case, a female in season can make a trip unenjoyable for dogs as well as humans. If you must hike with a female in heat, the combination of a feminine hygiene spray (sprayed on her bloomers, in the FUR), and giving chlorophyll tablets can cut down on her odor. Chlorophyll can be purchased at a health food store or in the vitamin section at many larger drug stores. My Malamute females weigh eighty or so pounds. They are given one-half the human dose twice a day (making a single human dose in a twenty-four-hour day).

WILDLIFE

Wildlife must be considered when planning a trip with dogs. Sure, it's nice to see deer, but if you are hiking through a migration area at the peak of migration, it might be a bit hard on your arms with a dog that keeps wanting to follow a deer. "Look, Mom, a deer! Look, Mom, another deer!" The best-behaved dog will become animated at the sight of deer bounding away, and the same goes for range cattle.

Bears are another matter altogether. If you are hiking in bear country, I cannot stress enough the importance of keeping a CLEAN CAMP. Take any and all precautions to avoid attracting bears, including stashing food in a tree outside of camp. I make the dogs sleep in the tent with me in bear country. In most places bears will not bother you, but some bears are not afraid of people.

Marmots and raccoons—you know, those cute furry critters that live in the woods—can also be a problem. Marmots are the ones that whistle when you come too close, just before they disappear into their safe holes. Some designated campsites will have Marmot poles so you can suspend your food over air. I tend to suspend the food over the dog(s).

Snakes are an issue as well. I am pleased that there are successful, humane ways to train your hiking companions to avoid snakes. You can enroll them in a snake avoidance clinic. I have several friends who have put multiple dogs through these clinics. Two have dogs that would have been bitten by rattlesnakes if they had not been trained to avoid snakes. One friend had snakes go into the kennel area with her dogs on multiple occasions. The other met snakes on the trail. Both were extremely happy with the reactions of their dogs trained to avoid, AVOID. On the Internet, www.patrickcallaghan.com is one place to check out snake avoidance clinics. The clinics use real snakes and are called Rattlesnake Avoidance Training. This site specializes in training dogs, cats, horses, and llamas.

Don't let this information frighten you. Simply be prepared. Mother Nature will always have something new for you on the trail. Preparation can mean the difference between success and disaster.

ANYTHING ELSE?

When planning a long trip, don't leave out sight-seeing. If you are going to be within a few miles of some special area, it is okay for you and your dog to catch a ride! Rent a car. Rent a bicycle. Enjoy the trip. See it all!

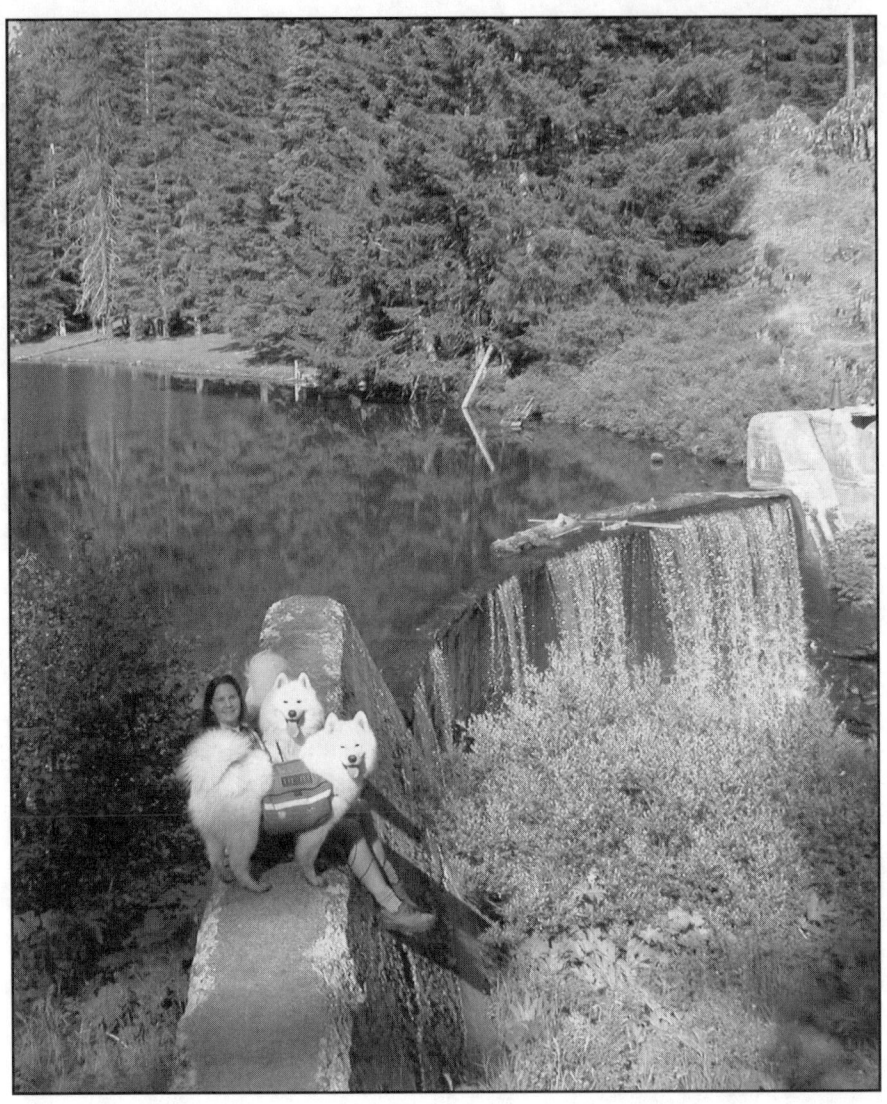

Take time to stop and enjoy the scenery. Linda von Hanneken-Martin relaxes during a trek with her two Samoyeds. Photo by Paul Martin.

Geocaching:
A Fun Way to Hike Locally with Dogs

Geocaching—pronounced GEE-o-cashing—is a growing sport for "children of adult age". Basically, geocaching is a cross between a treasure hunt and hide-and-seek, in which participants hide treasures, or caches, all over the globe. You search for "buried treasure" using high-tech gadgets with no chance of encountering pirates or other hostile creatures.

Folks who like to geocache ("cachers" for short) are of all ages, shapes and sizes. (One woman was having so much fun, she lost over fifty pounds in one year—all because she was up and out looking for caches.) For those who like to get out with their dogs, this makes for a fun trip. Put your cache items in your dog's pack, take a lunch, and set out for some fun. Your dog may even be able to help you locate the cache—his nose is far superior to your sight when it comes to locating an unusual object along your route.

The website www.geocaching.com is the site to visit for this sport. Fill in your zip code (or a state or country) into the search field and you will get a list of caches within 100 miles. The caches will have names, hints, descriptions, and the GPS coordinates in longitude and latitude. You will get a list of dozens, or even hundreds, of caches. Many may be within a very short distance of the zip code you entered.

The sport is basic; rules are simple:

1. Locate the cache, trying to not bee seen.
2. Take something from the cache.
3. Leave something in the cache.
4. Write about it in the cache's log book.
5. Log your success onto the web page.

WHAT IS IN A CACHE?

Caches are "treasures" that have been stashed almost anywhere on the planet. Sometimes they are in cups or plastic containers. Originally many caches were placed in metal ammunition boxes to better protect the contents from the elements. Toys, puzzles, and trinkets worth a few dollars are items commonly found in caches. One cache, about the size of a film canister, was stuck to the bottom of a public telephone. Some of the caches might even be "virtual." A box or container won't be hidden there. So you have to take a picture to claim a virtual cache. Sometimes the cache is hidden in plain sight. Some are so obvious they take longer to find.

WHO LEAVES CACHES?

Anyone can leave a cache for others cachers to find. There is even a name for non-gamers. They are called Muggles (borrowed from Harry Potter). It is suggested that when leaving a cache, you place a note inside congratulating the Muggles for their discovery, game play instructions, and a suggestion that they join the fun by visiting www.geocaching.com. You should also include contact information, e-mail or a phone number. Basically, leave information for Muggles to verify that this is not a dangerous item. Also ask them to please leave the cache intact where it was found. Who knows, the Muggle that finds a cache accidentally might become interested in joining the fun. Remember, when looking for a cache it's not good form to allow Muggles that may be in the vicinity to know you are looking. It's all part of the fun.

HOW TO START

The first steps in playing the game are relatively easy. You browse the descriptions of caches and choose which cache you want to locate. Armed with a GPS unit (a device that uses satellite signals to fix location anywhere on the planet, give or take fifteen to twenty feet) and an item to leave in the cache when you find it, you set out on your adventure.

A GPS unit is recommended, but it is not required. Latitude and longitude are provided in two formats—World Geodetic System

1984 for GPS units and Universal Transverse Mercator coordinates for topographical or street maps. Using map coordinates is less precise and makes the search more difficult.

The price of GPS units has dropped drastically in the last few years. Some cars are set up with GPS units. Handheld GPS systems, which cost as low as $100, can be the size of cell phones. The low price of handheld GPSs and ease of Internet access have fueled this truly fast-growing hobby/sport.

LEAVING YOUR OWN CACHE

If you do decide to leave your own cache, you should be sensitive to what and where you leave the cache as well as what you use for a cache container. You shouldn't place anything you wouldn't want a ten-year-old to find in your cache if it's in a public park where small children might happen upon it. One cache was on land that, although publicly used, was maintained by a private citizen. When the caretaker found the spray-painted ammo box, he called the police. Luckily, the 911 operator was a geocacher, so she knew not to send out the bomb squad.

Still, several municipalities have banned geocaching, not because the hunt could endanger cachers, but because the caches themselves could prove a danger. Since the coordinates are posted in a public forum, anyone has access to the cache and could put anything in the cache he wishes. Officials worried that a person could put a harmful substance in a cache, and the next cacher could be injured. They worried that the city could be liable if a lawsuit were filed.

Because of these concerns, the geocache website has since clarified that caches should always be on designated trails, never buried, and not cached beside active railroad tracks or under public structures deemed targets for terrorist attacks. They have even gone as far as to enlist a group of ten volunteers to approve new cache postings and check for accuracy.

Still, some complaints surfaced when cachers used ammunition boxes. After September 11, park rangers and Muggles weren't thrilled about finding abandoned ammo containers lying around. Since then cachers have started using sealable plastic containers like Tupperware/Rubbermaid or similar containers. They clearly label them as a geocache and include an explanation of the sport.

Listing a contact phone number or e-mail address with the cache log is now the norm.

Being the first person to find a cache is something very special and cachers race to be the first to get to a new cache. Imagine being ten minutes behind the first one to find a new cache. Many cachers have a stamp they use as their signature. If you read the logs on the geocaching web site, next to the name is the number of caches that person has found. Some people have numbers in the hundreds; some have over a thousand.

Some cachers have set up multi-cache hunts. To complete the hunt, cachers are required to solve trivia questions and math problems at multiple locations. The answers will give cachers the missing GPS coordinates to the treasure. Lists of clues, as well as instructions directing them to a starting point, are posted online. The cacher would need both a GPS unit and word-problem solving skills to find the treasure.

A LITTLE HISTORY

Dave Ulmer hid the first cache near Portland, Oregon, on May 3, 2000. This was his response to the government's lifting of "select availability" of the previously restricted signal for the Global Positioning System (GPS). Mike Teague found the cache and designed a web page to keep track of it. Three days later, it had been found twice.

Teague was contacted by Jeremy Irish in July 2000. Irish persuaded Teague to undertake a partnership and together they formed www.geocaching.com. Irish has developed and maintained the award-winning website since its September 2000 launch and now runs the website with Bryan Roth.

WHY IS GEOCACHING IN THIS BOOK?

Caching has motivated many individuals to get up and get out of the house. Taking a four-legged hiking companion fits right in with this new sport. It is yet another way to spend some quality time with your dog. You can spend anywhere from a couple of hours to days when caching. It is also a way to learn more about your local community and the surrounding areas.

Appendix

THE DOGPACKER'S CHECKLIST

I hope you will find the following checklist helpful. I use it to remind myself of important tasks, and also when planning my trip.

Before You Start
- Pick up all permits, including wilderness and fire.
- Find out the currect fire danger level.
- Check the status of surface and other water sources.
- Check local weather.

When You Arrive in Camp
- Pick a nice place to stop and rest or camp.
- Stake out the dogs.
- Give dogs water (and food if it's mealtime).
- Let dogs rest or sleep. (Most dogs will sleep after arriving in camp. Let them. They usually sleep an hour or two).
- Filter water and collect firewood. This is easiest when there is still daylight.
- Set up camp.
- Feed dogs (if you haven't already done so).
- Prepare and eat dinner.
- Wash dishes.

Just Before Bedtime
- Walk dogs.
- Secure dogs for the night.
- Secure camp for the night.

In the Morning
- Feed and water dogs. (I heat the dog food and water if the weather is cold.)
- Eat a good breakfast.
- Pack up camp.
- Clean up any "night deposits" the dogs have made.
- Put on your own and your dog's packs.
- Check camp to see that you have not forgotten anything.

On the Trail
- Have a great time hiking.
- Take care of yourself.
- Take care of your dogs. (In this order. If something happens to you, who will take care of the dogs?)

For Further Information

GROUPS THAT OFFER A PACK DOG CERTIFICATE

All breed:
    Alaskan Malamute Help League
        http://www.malamuterescue.com/workingdog.html/
    Canine Backpackers Association
        http://www.caninebackpackers.org/
    Dog Scouts of America
        http://www.dogscouts.com/

Breed specific:
    Alaskan Malamute Club of America
        http://www.alaskanmalamute.org/workgam.htm
    Collies (members only)
        http://www.awca.net/progs.htm/
    Greater Swiss Mountain Dog
        http://www.gsmdca.org/
    Samoyed Working Dogs
        http://www.samoyed.org/WorkDog.html/
    Siberian Husky Club of America
        http://www.shca.org/shcahp6e.htm/

E-mail groups:
    Canine Backpackers Association
        http://www.caninebackpackers.org/
    Sleddog Central (great resource)
        http://www.sleddogcentral.com/
    Trail Dog E-mail List
        If you want to join, just go to Yahoo Groups
        http://www.groups.yahoo.com/

CLUBS AND ORGANIZATIONS

ATC's Dogs on the Trail–Appalachian Trail Conference
    http://www.appalachiantrail.org/
Canine Backpackers Association
    http://www.caninebackpackers.org/
Federation of Western Outdoor Clubs
    http://www.federationofwesternoutdoorclubs.org/
FIDOS (Friends Interested in Dogs and Open Space)
    http://www.fidos.org/
Lewis & Clark Trail Heritage Foundation
    http://www.lewisandclark.org/
New England Trails Conference
    http://www.wapack.org/netrails/

MANUFACTURERS AND SUPPLIERS

Alpine Outfitters
P.O. Box 1728, Marysville, WA 98270
http://www.alpineoutfitters.net/
phone: 360-659-3800
e-mail: sales@AlpineOutfitters.net

Black Ice Dog Sledding Equipment
3620 Yancy Ave, New Germany, MN 55367
http://www.blackicedogsledding.com/
phone: 320-485-4825
e-mail: shilon@tds.net

Black Star Kennels
P.O. Box 22333, Minneapolis, MN 55422-0333
http://www.blackstars.biz/
phone: 1-866-DOG-SLED and 1-877-DOG-CART
e-mail: Tom@blackstars.biz

Chinookwind Outfitters
P.O. Box 218, Conifer, CO, 80433
http://www.chinookwind.com/
phone: 866-626-1099 (toll free) or in CO 303-679-9497
e-mail: dogsport@chinookwind.com

Eagle Creek Packs
3055 Enterprise Court, Vista, CA 92083
http://www.eaglecreek.com/
phone: 1-800-874-1048

Expedition Outfitters
San Jose, CA
http://www.expeditionoutfittersonline.com/
e-mail: merchandise@expeditionsamoyeds.org

Frostline Kits
2525 River Road, Grand Junction, CO 81505
http://www.frostlinekits.com

Granite Gear
P.O. Box 278, Two Harbors, MN 55616
http://www.granitegear.com/

Ikon Outfitters Ltd.
7597 Latham Road, Lodi, WI 53555-9526
http://www.ikonoutfitters.com/
phone: 608-592-4397

Mountainsmith Dog Packs
Heritage Sq. Bldg P, 18301 N. Colfax, Golden, CO 80401
http://www.mountainsmith.com/

Nordkyn Outfitters
P.O. Box 1023, Graham, WA 98338
http://www.nordkyn.com/packs.htm
phone: 1-800-326-4128 (for orders only), 253-847-4128 (for info)
e-mail: nordkyn@nordkyn.com

Perry Greene Outfitters
449 Atlantic Highway, Route 1, Waldoboro, ME 04572
http://www.mainely-dogs.com/
phone: 207-832-5227
e-mail: info@mainely-dogs.com

Rae's Harness Shop
549 West Intl Airport Road, # B10, Anchorage, AK 99518
http://www.raesharness.com/
phone: 1-800-770-1177(for orders only), 907-563-3411 (for info)

Ruff Wear Packs
P.O. Box 1363, Bend, OR 97709
http://www.ruffwear.com/
phone: 888-783-3932
e-mail: luckydog@ruffwear.com

Toneeka Outfitters
6229 Gunter Way, San Jose, CA 95123
phone: 408-365-0934

Trailhound Gearshop
63 Brook Street, Asheville, NC 28803
http://www.trailhound.com/
phone: 1-866-DOG-PACK (1-866-364-7225) Local: 828-274-3335
e-mail: jay@trailhound.com

Tun-Dra Outfitters
16438 96th Ave., Nunica, MI 49448
phone: 616-837-9726

Wenaha Dog Packs
5274 State Route 9, Sedro Woolley, WA 98284
phone: 1-800-917-0707
e-mail: wenaha4@aol.com

Wolf Packs, Inc.
1940 Soda Mountain Road, # I, Ashland, OR 97520
http://www.wolfpacks.com/
phone: 541-482-7669

Australian manufacturer and supplier of canine backpacks:
Windchill Dog Gear
Ralph and Sandy Koch
P.O. Box 41, Hurstbridge VIC 3099, Australia
http://www.windchill.com.au
phone: 61 3 9714 8540
e-mail: windchill@bigpond.com.au

WEBSITES

Sleddog Central (more info than you can use, a great resource)
http://www.sleddogcentral.com/

Geocaching (for information on a cache site near you)
http://www.geocaching.com

MAGAZINES THAT FEATURE ARTICLES ON BACKPACKING

Backpacker: The Magazine of Wilderness Travel
Rodale Press, Inc.
33 E. Minor Street, Emmaus, PA 18098
http://www.backpacker.com/

Dog Fancy
Subscription Service
P.O. Box 53264, Boulder, CO 80322
http://www.dogfancy.com/

Dog World Magazine
Primedia Publications
29 North Wacker Drive, Chicago, IL 60606-3298
http://www.dogworldmag.com/

Mushing
P.O. Box 149, Ester, AK 99725
http://www.mushing.com/

Purebred Dogs, The American Kennel Club Gazette
5580 Centerview Drive, Raleigh, NC 27690-0643
http://www.akc.org/pubs/gazette

Index

age, for packing, 33
Alaskan Malamute, 1, 3, 5, 8, 10, 18, 22, 86, 91
Alaskan Malamute Club of America, 82-83, 103
"working titles," 103
Appalachian Trail, 79, 81

backpacking, with dogs
　advantages of, 1-2
　as a working title, v
　damage to environment, 2
biking, mountain, 75-78
　guidelines for, 75-76
　preparing for, 76-78
Bizz Johnson Trail (CA), 35
booties, 91, 92-93
breakfast items, 47, 83, 102
breeds, that can pack, 3
Bureau of Land Management (BLM), 35, 36, 43

campfire permits, 43
chairs, for packing, 56
chicken and dumplings (recipe), 50
chicken, roasted, 49
coats, of dogs and packing, 3
collars, for packing, 5
color, of packs, 16
communication, 87

Companion Dog program, 38
conditioning, 21-31, 87
courtesy, importance of, 3
cross-country hiking, 36, 87-89
Dalmatians, 15
dayhiking, 1
Davenport, Kathi and Paul, 25
Death Valley, 34
dehydration, avoiding, 69
　checking for, 69
dinner items, 49, 83, 101
dog pack, 5, *see also* packs, dog
dogpacker's checklist, 79-80
dog pack manufacturers, 104-107
dog pack suppliers, 104-107

equipment, for dog backpacking, 5-6, 55-57
　dog necessities, 55
　overnight necessities, 55-57

Fahs, Barb, 4
fasteners, for packs, 12-13, 14
Fastex fasteners, 13, 14
female cycles (menstruation and heat), 91, 94
Fennell, Lisa, 32
fire hazards, 43
first aid kits, 55, 58, 70
flea collars, 55
Flexi Leads, 5

food poisoning, 91
foot care, for your dog, 41
freezer bags, for packing, 60
frost bite, 74

geocaching, 97-100
German Shepherds, 25
giardia, 51
Global Positioning System
 (GPS), 100
Golden Retrievers, 24
Guide to Our Federal Lands, 35

Hacker, Mike, 2, 31
health, of your dog, 40-43
heartworms, 40
heat cramps, 70
heat exhaustion, 74
heat stroke, 74
herding breeds, 4
hiking organizations, 104
hiking with dogs,
 nine rules for, 72
Hutcherson, Phil and Laura, 37
hypothermia, 74

insects, 66
introduction, of pack to dog,
 22-26
Irish, Jeremy, 100
Ivey, Mindy, 27

John Muir Wilderness, 37
Jorgenson, Kirt, 71
Julian family, 22

LaBelle, Charlene and Steve, 64
"landmines," 45,72
Larkins, D. and M., 62

Lassen National Forest, 64
leashes, for packing, 5
livestock, and dogs, 72
logging in (and out), 65
logging roads, 36
lunch items, 47-48
Lyme disease, 40

Magee, Becky, 73
Malamute Quarterly, v
manners, on the trail, 29-31,
 65-66
Martin, Paul and Linda, 81, 96
McCracy, Sharon, 62
meal planning, 45-54
 dog meals, 45, 48, 49, 83
 matrix for, 47
 people meals, 45-47, 83

nail care, for your dog, 41-42,
 87, 91, 93
nail protection, for tent, 91
Nakashima, Dale, 44
national forests, 35, 37
national monuments, 38
national parks, 35, 38, 67, 81
Neat Sheet, 89, 90
Nichols, Mona, 44
Northern California Alaskan
 Malamute Association
 (NCAMA), v, 64

obedience training, for
 packing, 21
one-piece packs, 8-10, 9
overnighters, 1, 3

Pacific Crest Trail, 35, 79
packaging, of food, 46

packing breed dogs, 3, 5
packing by size, shape, and
    weight, 60
packs, dog
    cost of, 8
    contour, 7, 8, 12
    definition of, 7
    features of a well-
        constructed pack, 19
    fitting and placement of,
        16-20
    how to choose, 7-20
    how to pack, 57, 59, 60, 61,
        62-63
    importance of fitting
        properly, 8, 16
    manufacturers of, 104-107
    one-piece, 8-10, 9
    saddlebag/"U", 7, 8
    square/box, 7, 8, 11
    suppliers, 104-107
    two-piece, 10-12
    types of, 8-12
    where to buy, 7
pads, care of dog's feet, 42-43
pads, for packing, 10, 11, 83
Palazzari, Vikki and John, viii
Palmer, Glen and Vicky, 64
panniers, 10
parks, for packing, 36
Pensock, John, 24
permission, 43
permits, 37, 43, 82
Perry, Mike, 64
Pine Crest Trail (CA), 30
planning, trip, 33-43, 79
preparations, trip, 33-34
private property, 37-38, 43
publications, for dogpacking, 107

reactions, of the dog, 65
recipes, for packing, 49-50
"refresh stops," 67
repellent, insect, 55, 66
roads, for packing,
    see also trails, for hiking
rope, for securing dog, 55, 73
Roth, Bryan, 100
Rottweilers, 3, 32
routes, planning, 38-40
rules for hiking with dogs, 72

safety tips, 20
Samoyed, 91, 96
Seal-a-Meal containers, 45
Sierra Nevada Forest, 37
Siberian Husky, 85, 91
sledding, v
snacks, 45, 49, 55
sources, for hiking trails, 35-38
    bookstores, 35
    libraries, 35
    outdoor stores, 35
    pamphlets, 35
sporting breeds, 4
straps, for packs, 12-13-15
    brush straps, 13, 15
supplies, survival, 60
    things to take, 83-84, 86
support, while traveling, 85
Susanville (CA), 35

tannic acid, for foot care, 42-43
Teague, Mike, 100
temperatures, extreme, 70
tie-outs, 55
topographical (TOPO) maps,
    38, 39, 80, 81
towel training, 22

trails, for hiking, 34-38
    fire roads, 36
    historical, 36
    jeep trails, 36
    jogging, 36
    logging roads, 36
    parks, county, city, state, 36
trails, types of, 3, 79-80
training, importance of, vi, 22
    where your dog can walk;
        behind you, 28-29
        beside you, 26-28, 27
        in front, 26, 27

training walks, 24-26
trash, removal of, 66, 86
treating water, 54
trips, planning your first, 33-43
two-piece packs, 10-12, 11

U.S. Geological Survey, 38
U.S. Postal Service (or USPS), 84, 87

vaccination records, 40, 55

wading, for sore feet, 68, 71
walking sticks, 56
water, 51-54, 55
    boiling, 54
    basins, 57
    crossings, 87, 88
    containers for, 51, 52, 57
    filters for, 51-52, 53
    ice water tips, 70
    stops, 67-68
    treating, 52, 54
weather, and trips, 34, 70
websites, 107

weight, for training, 23
    pulling, v
    that a dog can carry, 5
Wenaja Dog Packs, 15
Westwood (CA), 35
Whitney Peak, (CA), vi, 28
wilderness permits, 43
wildlife, 94
working dogs, 4
working title, v
    groups that offer, 103

yokes, 10-12, 20